Women in the Qur'an:
An Emancipatory Reading

Asma Lamrabet

Translated by Myriam Francois-Cerrah

Square View

This book has been selected to receive financial assistance from English PEN's "PEN Translates!" programme, supported by Arts Council England. English PEN exists to promote literature and our understanding of it, to uphold writers' freedoms around the world, to campaign against the persecution and imprisonment of writers for stating their views, and to promote the friendly co-operation of writers and the free exchange of ideas. **www.englishpen.org**

Women in the Qur'an: An Emancipatory Reading

First published in England by Square View, 2016
6th impression, 2021
Distributed by Kube Publishing Ltd
Markfield Conference Centre
Ratby Lane, Markfield,
Leicestershire LE67 9SY
United Kingdom
Tel: +44 (0) 1530 249230
Fax: +44 (0) 1530 249656
Website: www.kubepublishing.com
Email: info@kubepublishing.com

CIP data for this book is available from the British Library.

ISBN 978-0-99351-660-3 *casebound*
ISBN 978-0-99351-661-0 *paperback*
ISBN 978-0-99351-662-7 *ebook*

Cover design: Fatima Jamadar
Book design/Typesetting: Nasir Cadir

Printed by Elma Basim, Istanbul, Turkey

CONTENTS

PART ONE

PART TWO

ᘛᘔᘕᘔᘚ

PREFACE TO THE ENGLISH EDITION

Knowledge is power; and, like power, it can be used to serve diametrically opposed objectives: from serving humanity, to the destruction of what is good for mankind. Hence, the need for sound understanding and informed discussion.

Islam today is perhaps the world's most discussed religion; yet, arguably its most misunderstood one. Islamophobia and contrived efforts to impose reforms from outside or engineer them from within, have only aggravated the situation. Nevertheless, it may be worthwhile for both Islam's advocates and adversaries to revisit their positions and explore avenues of real understanding through reflection and dialogue, as opposed to blind advocacy or outright demonization.

Square View is not a commercial imprint in the traditional market. Its aim is to make available to the readers, Muslim and non-Muslim, male and female, young and old, literature that may enable them to appreciate Islam and Muslim life, history and culture, *as Muslims understand them*. This understanding is based on and rooted in the sources that Muslims hold to be authentic, enduring and inviolable. Yet it also reflects the genuine plurality that characterises the historical and contemporary intellectual landscape of the world of Islam. The Qur'an, as the Word of God is the primary and eternal source of the Islamic vision of life and human destiny. The Sunnah of the Prophet Muhammad (peace be upon him) is the model for individual and collective behaviour for all times to come. *Fiqh*, developed in the light of these primary sources, provides a practical framework for individual and collective life and behaviour. This framework has a built-in mechanism to cater for the demands of permanence and change. It is not monolithic. Various schools of thought reflect the plurality of human endeavours to live in accordance with the values and principles of Islam in a variety of contexts. Islamic history showcases these endeavours of applying the guidance provided in the original sources of the Qur'an and Sunnah to problems and challenges as they have arisen in different times and climes. *Tafsir* literature reflects similar efforts to understand the Divine message and seek its application to changing and evolving situations. Loyalty to the sources, and a disciplined effort to apply the eternal guidance of scripture to temporal situations, is the hallmark of the Muslim intellectual enterprise, spread over almost a millennium and a half. Movements towards reform, revival and reconstruction, drawing upon the internal sources, constitute, despite their diversity and at times apparent conflict, a source of strength. They are an integral part of the historical process. The conscience of the Muslim ummah has welcomed and assimilated reforms and changes which it found to be in consonance with the letter and spirit of Divine guidance and rejected and spurned what it found to be incongruent and inconsistent with the same. External influences have also played their role. There have been trends that represented deviations and departures from the norm. Nonetheless, only that has been acceptable to the Ummah which it deemed authentic and which emerged as part of an internal process, resulting in continuity with change and variety. Respect for Islamic hermeneutic principles, as found in the fields of *tafsir* and *usul-al-fiqh*, has ensured the proper following of this process.

The editorial policy pursued by Square View is consistent with this tradition of Islamic scholarship. The views expressed in the books and monographs published by Square View represent the views of their authors and not necessarily the views of the publishing house or the sponsoring research institutions. We believe that healthy discussion to promote a better understanding of Islam and Muslim history, respecting the integrity and authenticity of the sources along with an opportunity to differ, discuss and innovate within the Islamic tradition is the path that leads to the development of knowledge in the service of Islamic ideals.

It is in this spirit that we are publishing the English translation of Asma Lamrabet's book: *Women in the Qur'an: An Emancipatory Reading*. This is a work of engaged scholarship looking upon the place and role of women in Islam. The author is an accomplished Moroccan Islamic activist and has tried to meticulously study the Qur'an albeit from a fresh perspective. Her original work had been reviewed, revised and corrected by Dr. Ahmed Abaddi, Secretary General of Rabita Mohammadia of Ulema's of Morocco. Many may disagree with her findings, formulations and interpretations as she has differed from some of the accomplished interpretations of her predecessors. Agreement with all past interpretations is not the real issue. What is to be seen is whether an effort has been made to look at the Revealed Text with a spirit of loyalty and faith in the Divine Authority, while earnestly searching for solutions to new problems within the matrix of Divine Guidance.

Lamrabet's work is a radical reinterpretation of the Islamic tradition based on scripture. This is to be praised inasmuch as it is a sincere attempt at bringing the Islamic tradition into conversation with contemporary concerns. Such attempts at remaining true to scripture in light of the changing conditions in which Muslims live, brought about by modernity, are essential to keeping Islam a vibrant religious system. However, some of Lamrabet's interpretations are quite daring, and will no doubt be seen as problematic. Among other issues, it is unfortunate that there appears to be a general disregard for the hadith corpus, which must be engaged seriously and respectfully if one is to do justice to the sensitive topics under discussion.

Lamrabet's sweeping judgements regarding "traditionalist" understanding of Islam, by which she seems to be referring to the scholastic tradition of the past fourteen hundred years, are unfortunately not always substantiated in her work. Rather they are left as broad claims. In attempting to remedy this to some degree, we have included some endnotes. While Square View does not necessarily endorse all the ideas in this work, we hope that the work will provoke a much needed critical engagement with it, and more broadly with modernity and the pre-modern Islamic tradition in light of both the Qur'an and the Sunnah. As a first step in that direction, Lamrabet's work makes a valuable contribution.

The present work is being presented to the English reading public with a view to providing access to some trends in contemporary Muslim thinking. The original book was published in French and has run into several editions. The English edition has been ably rendered by Myriam Francois-Cerrah. Every effort has been made to adhere faithfully to the author's grammatical and typographical style. Our former commissioning editor Yahya Birt initiated the process which was meticulously completed by his successor Dr. Muhammad Siddique Seddon. We are thankful to both of them for their valuable contribution towards the editing of the present work. We are also grateful to PEN for awarding us the 'Winner of an English PEN Award' and for a grant towards the translation of this thought-provoking work.

The Publisher
January 2016

INTRODUCING THE AUTHOR

A meeting with very special Muslim women
The Parisian suburbs ... . Saint-Denis, Sartrouville, the Yvelines ... .
Neighbourhoods which I know only by name. It is grey and cold, despite it being springtime. Housing project tower blocks where generations of immigrants are expected to flourish ... . A sad setting.

Luckily, there was this meeting, those smiles ... . a glimmer of hope in this grey French sky. These Muslim women from over there ... . True members of the resistance.

They are there, welcoming me with lots of expectation, a certain shyness, a hint of curiosity ... . For them I probably represent the other part of themselves, the one from back home, from the roots, the source.

The other side of the Mediterranean from where, ultimately, everything comes, where this idealized Islam lives ... . Of course, since it is at home there. This allegedly calm Islam they call home, where they so wish they could live sometimes, especially at difficult times such as these when it is not easy living here, when one self describes and wishes to be Muslim ... . and especially a Muslim woman.

Apparently, I am like a breath of fresh air to them, as one of them tells me. But if they only knew. If they only knew that it is them who have dazzled me, with their energy, their wisdom, their lucidity ... .

Still very young for the most part, they each have a journey which betrays a profound maturity of mind ... . By force of circumstances, we emerge grown from life's struggles. And in fact, one discerns on their faces, in their smiles and in their expressions, the deep impact of so many life struggles ... .

How many life experiences, stories and journeys, where the act of living one's faith daily becomes an incessant struggle and an experience of being truly torn ... . But how much dignity also, how much realism and humility!

Their struggle? It is on all fronts. To face an environment increasingly hostile to their need for spirituality, to struggle against all forms of discrimination, to assert their right to be fully fledged citizens, to denounce the politics of marginalisation which consistently relegates them to an eternal sub-culture.

Despite the multiple challenges, they do not give up. And as one of them said to me, 'each conflict we experience enriches us and highlights our shortcomings and weaknesses. It pushes us at the same time to think, to improve and to try and surpass ourselves.'

True warriors ... .

They are continuously searching for a sense of well-being despite other people's stares, each day a little more aggressive.

Nonetheless, it is sometimes other people's stares which have led them to question themselves and to rework their spirituality in order, in fact, to better themselves ... .

They dream of living their Islam peacefully. They dream of a serene and free spirituality ... .

But every aspect of their daily life amounts to facing a growing animosity against their spiritual identity. They have learned to live with their Islam, as one learns to live with an intractable and profound chronic illness.

A recurring pain following almost daily politico-media indictments. They dream of reformism, of renewal, of remaking the world. Their world.

But the observation of a fossilized traditionalism is obvious in their surroundings and at the heart of a community which is desperately seeking itself.

The debate is passionate, frenetic. But it is also of a high intellectual calibre, because the demands are legitimate and the critiques merited, in the face of the archaic daily lives of Muslims .... They do not want to live Islam merely with their hearts, but also with their minds.

Passionate, they clearly are, but beyond this impassioned Islam which they experience with their heart, their quest for spirituality is also a quest for meaning and recognition.

It is what enables them to get through often very complex social situations with a lot of realism and discernment .... .

Their work on the ground is impressive but remains insufficient in their eyes and as one reminded me: 'Beyond a new Muslim intellectual theorising, which has already begun, it is its implementation on the ground which is imperatively required right now!'

Their motto? An unwavering commitment to their faith, their identity, but also to their French citizenship which they wish to experience fully ... without caveats and particularly without political blackmail! Conscious that the debate concerning the veil, women and Islam is merely a political-media strategy which seeks above all else to instrumentalize them in order to better stigmatize them.

They have moved beyond the stage of an identity crisis which means one feels torn between two apparently irreconcilable cultures.

Through their faith, they have already reconciled the two and wish moreover to define their own culture, diverse, fertile, open to all universal values.

How many challenges to overcome and paths to cross!? How many situations of self-denial, of struggles, of humiliations, of psychological barriers to confront, to undergo, to live through ... . ?

Will they have the courage to go through with it? The courage to not succumb to this nagging temptation to renounce, to resign, to abandon everything, like so many others.

Will they be allowed to accomplish their project: to live their Islam in harmony with a rights-based citizenship? Or will they be discouraged, pushed to their wits end and made hostages of an ideological confrontation of which the central implication is a covert racism.

I wish through these lines to express my admiration to them for their work ... . for their resistance, their struggle which somewhere along the lines is also my own. My sincere emotion at having known them, my desire to see them continue their activism ... . In particular, I want to tell them to hold on.

If things change in Islam today, it is also thanks to this substantive work, to this spirit of renewal, thanks to all these struggles ... . In Islamic or Western lands, it is the same breath of spirituality, of freedom and of hope, which stirs hearts and minds ... .

To these French Muslim women, I dedicate this book.

To these resistance figures in the shadows whom I met that certain spring in 2004 and who inspired me to undertake this re-reading which, I hope with much humility, will help them, however little, in their struggle ... .

To Zhor, Hanan, Malika, Nourhen, Khadija, Aloise, Naila, but also Amira, the Tunisian princess, Fatema, Aicha and all the others, whose names I do not recall but whose memories are indelibly engraved in my memory.

May God love you all.

THANKS

I wish to thank all those who read the more or less developed versions of my book and who enriched me through their previous advice, among them the members of the re-reading group in Rabat as well as all the members of the 'Presénce Musulmane Canada'. Thank you for your assistance, your sincerity and your encouragement .... .

I would like to thank in particular Mr Ahmed El Abbadi, Secretary General of the League of Ulema in Morocco, for taking the time to re-read this manuscript, to share his observations with me and his invaluable suggestions. I would like to thank him also for this kindness, his generosity and especially for his esteem and trust. Coming from a man known for his probity and intellectual integrity, I am touched and honoured.

I wouldn't know how to find the words for she who insisted on reading through page by page, to correct the innumerable errors, to question me, criticize me, thoroughly and conscientiously: Wafaa El Alami .... . thanks for your patience, your affection and your friendship.

To my brothers and sisters, with affection and tenderness .... . a particular mark of tenderness towards my little sister Zina. May God protect you and ensure you never weaken again in the face of injustice.

To my spiritual mother, Mrs Lamrabet Afif Fatéma. Thanks for teaching me so much .... .

INTRODUCTION

What kind of liberation are we speaking of?
For a long time, the question of the status of Muslim women has been taken hostage between two extreme interpretations: a very rigid conservative Islamic approach and a Western, Islamophobic and ethnocentric approach.

These two conceptions are of course at odds, but they share the same stumbling block: a dead-end. It is virtually impossible to conceive of even the hint of a debate to clarify certain points, given how blinded partisans from each perspective are by their respective certainties.

The Muslim woman, the victim of choice during centuries of stagnation and decadence, continues today to survive in a social system which perpetuates, of course to different degrees, oppression in the name of religion. This statement is rarely acknowledged in Muslim lands where often the *other* is incriminated for seeking to undermine, or even corrupt an entire social fabric of moral values, of which women are the main guarantor.

'Islam gave women all their rights ... It honours women ... It has protected them ...'. This is the favourite discourse of many Muslims, often very sincere, but whose arguments remain nevertheless very weak. A recurring discourse, constantly on the defensive, which is losing traction with time and which, for lack of convincing, is more revealing of a profound and manifest state of disarray.

We note in fact a patent anachronism between these two discourses and the lived reality which aims towards and claims to be respectful of Islamic values and in which the worst discriminations against women are justified ... From honour crimes to forced marriages, via retrograde laws which maintain women in the position of a minor for life, the list of injustices is long and remains unfortunately justified by a certain reading of Islam.

What is more, it is no secret that the status of women, such as it is conceived currently in traditionalist and dominant readings of Islam, remains the *obligatory* breach through which a certain Western hegemony continuously seeks to interfere in order to discredit an entire system of thought. The current meta-discourse on the *veiled, oppressed and reclusive* Muslim woman is merely a continuous reproduction of the orientalist and colonialist vision still in vogue in contemporary postcolonial representations.

This eternally accusatory discourse serves in particular as an alibi for all political attitudes of cultural domination and supports the binary analysis which pits, utterly unquestionably, the *universal* model of the *free* Western woman against that of the oppressed Muslim woman in need of *liberation* ... The opposition of these two models allows Muslim women to remain categorised as second-class citizens and in particular allows the image to be used as a *foil* in relation to modernity, civilization and freedom. It is ironic to note within a certain western discourse, which claims to be *liberating* and has *universalist* pretentions, the obvious signs of a language of paternalistic domination, which struggles to break with its colonial vocation of a *civilizing mission*. The desire is not to *free* Muslim women in order to simply free them, but rather to *showcase western freedom* and, thus, maintain the power relations which best enable domination of the other. It is not a question of demonizing the West and of accusing it of all ills. The contribution of western ideas to the long process of modernization is undeniable. But the critique is directed towards a certain strand of thinking which, in the name of its conception of the universal, claims to behold a monopoly on modernity and truth. It is not about denying the existence of a culture of oppression of women in Muslim lands but, rather, about denouncing what a given hegemonic western vision wishes to do to this culture by hyper-essentialising it. A Western perspective which maintains Muslim women in a one-dimensional grid in which they have been carefully enclosed and through which western values and norms are promoted as the only means of *liberating* those poor Muslim women.

Between these two diametrically opposed visions, the Muslim woman ultimately remains a prisoner, despite herself, of a discourse which in both cases, ignores her person, her aspirations and her will ... Between a frozen Islamic thought which assiduously *ring-fences* women's issues and a western ideology which takes pleasure from denigrating Islam through those same issues, one struggles to think of a third way, through which Muslim women can emerge from this ideological impasse.

The problem is that women and their status in Islam is a contentious subject and it would be difficult for anyone to deny this. But what is the truth of the matter? Is it truly religion, as a system of values, which oppresses us or a collective social reality which appropriates the religious in order to reformulate it according to a hierarchical representation which suits it and which allows it to better affirm its powers?

It is undeniable that when religion comes into being in an already sexually ascribed social order, it can only be absorbed into it, despite itself. It is also obvious that one is within one's right to question, and to remain perplexed in the face of the real contradiction which exists between the spiritual message of the Qur'an and the lived reality of Muslims. On one hand, Islam carries, like other monotheistic religions, a message of peace, love and justice, coming from a God who, in creating human beings, men and women, has made them unequivocally free, equal and dignified ... on the other hand, the traditionalist understanding of that same religion seems to contribute to a certain preponderance of men at the level of social reality and seems, therefore, to be one of the main vectors of discrimination against women. In a large number of interpretative readings of the Qur'an are found classic patterns of male domination where women are marginalized, even excluded in the name of the sacred ...[A] One can understand that the different religious interpretations can carry the imprint of the geopolitical contexts from which they emerge and of the socio-cultural environment which produced them. But it is harder to understand how, in the long term, these same interpretations have become themselves, immutable and entirely closed to all critical reflection. Interpretations which have removed the profound meaning of the message and which with time have become insurmountable barriers for those who wish to return to the *initial impulse* of the text and find within it answers to the needs of our time.

The confusion is such that it has become very difficult to distinguish between what is from the sacred text and what is from the domain of subjective human interpretation.

And yet, between the *humanist spirit* of the Qur'an which favours the human being *Insan*, without distinction according to gender, and certain classical interpretations demeaning towards women, there is a substantial misunderstanding which means that the lived reality of Muslims has become to this extent removed from their spiritual references.

The spiritual message is, as described by the Qur'an in several passages, a 'reminder' (*dhikr*) which consists in awakening in human beings the most noble side of their conscience in order that they remain in a continuous state of *proximity* with the Creator. And through this *remembrance*, there is an intimate conviction in Divine justice ... Nothing in the Qur'anic text can justify or support any sort of discrimination against women. It is this conviction which stems from profound faith but which truly struggles to materialize in our Muslim reality, which needs to be reformulated and put into practise on the ground, in daily life.

It is here that Islamic thought needs to evolve, in order to redefine itself, to be re-thought and to make the necessary distinction between the spiritual message and some interpretations which have fixed the text and at times, killed discussion.

This is what is happening, God willing, today in the Muslim world where the premises of a serene and well-thought through change are beginning to appear.

Despite an overall chaotic general assessment in the Muslim world, one discerns the clear though timid emergence of an innovating discourse, which seeks to *reform* religious thought that is currently dwindling and virtually entirely focused on its moralising tendency.

In fact, it is comforting to note the current emergence of an Islamic trend, albeit still marginal, which whilst still trying to find itself contributes to redrawing new spaces where the religious debate can evolve without losing its soul ....

Within these new spheres of reflection, that concerning the status of women in Islam is taking shape and affirming itself day by day. The question of women in Islam has always been at the heart of the debate, possibly even of all debates in the Islamic world. However, what is currently new is that at the heart of this intellectual effervescence, Muslim women are trying to *reclaim* their voice, in order to *re-appropriate* what has persistently remained in the hands of men, namely their own destiny!

Indeed today many intellectual Muslim women, living in Muslim societies but also in the West, through their academic research, social and theological, and particularly in the name of their faith, are questioning a significant amount of prejudice on this topic. They contest in particular a classical analysis which stipulates that the inequality between men and women and its corollary of discriminatory measures are an inherent part of the sacred text by demonstrating that, in fact, it is certain biased readings, bolstered by patriarchal customs, which have rather legitimated these same inequalities.

It is important to underline that these new positive forms of resistance are the prerogative of Muslim women who, whilst having a critical approach to certain religious readings, are practising believers and it is in the name of their faith that they assert their right to assess the text.

It is an effort to demarcate oneself from a women's movement coming from Muslims which seeks changes outside of the religious framework. Whilst one must respect this desire to define oneself outside of the religious framework, it is sad to note that these

Muslim women who are rebelling against the alleged *diktats* of the religion are those most heard and given the greatest amount of airtime ... This is not surprising in and of itself, since the only acceptable or even expected critique in Western circles today is that which challenges the Islamic tradition.[1]

What is original about this new form of female contestation in Islam which, it should be noted, is met with notable indifference in the West, is that it takes shape within and in the name of the Islamic tradition ... Muslim women who undertake, in the name of their convictions, a process of questioning of certain misogynistic readings in Islam and contest readings which legitimize the subordinate status of women in Islamic societies ... It is what some have referred to as *the questioners from within*. In fact, it is a project which is intrinsic to Qur'anic teachings and which advocates, in the very name of those teachings, the promotion of an egalitarian ethic both in theory and in practise.

It is thus at the heart of these debates and evolutions that the stake of a new reading of the sacred text lies ... A reading adapted to our context and to a human reality which never ceases to evolve. A reading which seeks to remain faithful to basic principles in Islam and which contends that the Qur'an is valid in all times and in all places.

How can we remain content with exegeses compiled centuries ago and which, concerning women, more often than not reflect a distressing literalism? Why do we continue to restrict ourselves to traditional readings when the text itself presents in its guiding principles extremely important latitudes so that each social reality can adapt to it and recognize itself within it. How can we remain with our arms crossed, regurgitating outmoded interpretations and hence ignoring the objectives of the text which, in every context,

---

1. One need look no further than the success of French editors publishing testimonies by Muslim women and the proposed titles which speak volumes on this obsession with representing the Muslim woman as an inevitable victim of Islam: *Burnt Alive* by Souad; *Forced to Marry* by Leila; *Mutilated* by Khady; *The Woman's Stoning* by Freidoune Sahebjam; *Disfigured* by Rania el Baz; *I Was Born in a Harem* by Choga Regina ... almost all of which were published in the year 2005 alone!

provides *meaning* to our life on earth? It is sad to note that instead of remaining faithful to the objectives of the Divine message, we have rather remained faithful to human interpretations and readings which, voluntarily or not, have contributed to the rise of this culture of demeaning women which continues to plague our Muslim societies.

It is in this sense that a re-reading of the Qur'an from a feminine perspective draws all its importance. It will enable us to create a true dynamic of liberation from within the Islamic sphere, in the sense of *raising the status* of Muslim women.

This *liberation reading* will also allow the development of a true autonomy and an authentic Islamic feminine identity with the totality of its rights and responsibilities. Finally, it will allow women to define themselves as active partners in the process of reform and religious reinterpretation which is underway in the Muslim world. Because one can, as a believer, question the assertion according to which only men have the authority to interpret what God has outlined in His Book.

This is not an attempt to promote a women-only hermeneutics which would exclude fourteen centuries of classical exegetical tradition. Classical exegesis constitutes a very rich patrimony for Islamic memory, its contribution is indeed critical for a profound study of the text and it is not about excluding the considerable contribution of this science for the understanding of the sacred text. Rather, it is about addressing historical prejudice and inequalities, driven by a human and hence imperfect understanding of the Qur'anic message. It is about *deconstructing* an entire patriarchal model of reading which relegates women to a corner of Islamic history, in order to return to women a part of their amputated memory.

It is certainly not about forging a movement which, coming from a female perspective, would seek to oppose women to men through a conflictual understanding ... this new feminine perspective questions the alleged male superiority but not on the basis of rivalry between the sexes. It is a new perspective which can only be enriching and which takes into account the spiritual experience of women, so often absent from the Islamic references. Spirituality has no gender, but there is a given lived relationship to God which is perceived differently by women and men ... It is here that the inclusion of the female perspective can be an *essential* addition to the human spiritual experience ... In addition, the Prophet of Islam (May Allah bless him and grant him peace) guided us from the beginning to conceiving of this female/male difference as a type of *equality at the heart of the fraternity in God* ... It is for this reason that at the heart of the Islamic reformist project, a number of Muslim men have for a long time been engaged in a process of re-reading and of liberation of women, according to the principles of Islam. This emanates precisely from a profound conviction in Divine justice and the absolute requirement of impartiality towards all human beings. Such conviction leads to a critical awakening in the believer, be it male or female, towards all the various forms of enslavement.

And refusing to endorse the subservience of which Muslim women are victims is itself an act of devotion, of piety and of faithfulness in front of the Creator.

It is of this *liberation* of which we speak ....

A *women's liberation* which advocates a spiritual rejuvenation through the Qur'an, Divine words, eternal, and an endless source of strength, of freedom and of hope ....

A *liberation* which favours above all else authenticity, the inner self and integrity.

A *liberation* which conceives of the relationship to transcendence as profoundly liberating since it frees us from all other forms of servitude ....

A *women's liberation* which does not have to conform to any other model in vogue, which is neither necessarily western, nor typically eastern, but autonomous and independent ....

A *women's liberation* which should be free to make its own choices, to re-write *its* history and to redefine *its* own spaces of freedom ....

A *liberation* well-grounded in its spiritual identity but which is open on all forms of human richness and is prepared to share with *others*, all *others*, the true universal values of ethics and justice ....

IN THE VERY BEGINNING ...

We must go back, way back, to the story of human creation ... The universal story and popular imagination are indelibly marked by a same and unique belief which transcends time, cultural space, religious dogma and the history of civilizations ... This belief stipulates that Adam - as a man - was God's first creation and that Eve, the woman, was created from one of Adam's ribs.

Henceforth, this legendary truth has become the founding myth of the inferiority of women and we know the disastrous effect this type of concept has had throughout the history of humanity.

It remains undeniable that the affirmation of the inferiority of women as compared to men finds its origins in theological assumptions widely anchored in ways of thinking, both in Judaeo-Christian cultures and in Muslim lands. Without going into the metaphysical details, these main assumptions are found, with much continuity, in the interpretative texts of the religious traditions of the three monotheistic religions and one can summarize the main points through three observations which continuously return in universal religious history.

Firstly, there is this idea that woman was created from Adam's rib, which equates to saying that her creation was necessarily secondary, Adam - man - being considered as the norm or representative of the human ideal.

The second observation is that which suggests that Eve is the primary cause of Adam's eviction from Paradise, since it is she, according to this very widespread understanding, who incited Adam to transgress God's command and to taste from the forbidden tree. She has become the undeniable muse of the legendary 'original sin'.

And the final assumption, that woman was not only created from Adam, but she was created *for* him! An important nuance! It is from here that the entire culture of the oppression of women that we are familiar with has emerged and which has found its legitimacy in a particular religious discourse. Today, the majority of Christian exegetes consider the story of Adam and Eve to be symbolic and many theologians interpret it differently from traditional readings. They recognize the existence of many contradictions in the Bible and reject classical interpretations which they consider to be too literalistic.

As for Islam, or, rather the Qur'anic text itself, nowhere does one find this conception of Eve coming from Adam's rib. Nonetheless, it is stupefying to see the extent to which the different commentaries and religious works, and moreover the Muslim imagination, have remained profoundly tainted by the traditionalist Judaeo-Christian understanding!

In the Qur'an, several verses illustrate a very different conception to that widely circulated nowadays. First we find a central verse in Surah *al Nisā'* (Women):

> O MANKIND! Be conscious of your Sustainer, who has created
> you out of one living entity, and out of it created its mate, and
> out of the two spread abroad a multitude of men and women [...]
> (*al Nisā'* 4: 1)[1]

It is very important to *redefine* the terminology used in the Qur'anic text concerning creation, because key words in this verse will be interpreted in the vast majority of cases according to a classical schema of the hierarchization of human creation. In fact, in classical commentaries the term *'nafs wahida'* refers to Adam as a masculine being and *zawj* to his wife.

---

1. Translation by Muhammed Asad.

However, a more structured approach indicates that the term '*nafs*', which is feminine in Arabic, refers to a range of notions which one can translate according to the meaning of the text, as: person, individual, soul, essence, matter, spirit, or even breath of life.

As for the term '*zawj*', it refers to both spouses, the pair or, the partner. It is often used to speak indistinguishably of the husband or wife and despite the fact it is grammatically masculine, it can be used both for the man or the woman.[2] In the Qur'an, it is often used to speak of a couple, and this, as much when discussing humans as plants or animals. It is what the Qur'an describes in this verse, for example:

> And in everything have We created pairs,[3] so that you might bear in mind [that God alone is One]. (al-Dhāriyāt 51: 49) [4]

Nevertheless, a great majority of scholars interpret the term '*nafs*' as 'Adam' as a man or male and the term *zawj* as 'wife', which, according to this logic, reinforces the classical anthropomorphic representation of the origin of human creation. Since Adam is a man, the term '*zawj*', as referred to by the Qur'an in this verse, refers to the female counterpart, namely Eve or Hawwa. Since the first exegetes drew widely from the pre-Islamic religious heritage in order to support their interpretations, the legend of the creation of Eve from Adam's rib was widely reported and subsequently endorsed by Muslim scholars.

Starting from this assumption and certain supporting hadiths, the classical commentators concluded that Eve was created from one of Adam's ribs.

However, one notes firstly that in the Qur'an, Eve (or Hawwa) is not mentioned by her name. The significance of the term '*zawj*' or 'partner' depends on the meaning of the verse or '*siyaq al-ayah*'. Based on the consistency and the orientation of the verse, the term

---

2. The term '*zawj*' is used in the Qur'an to refer to both the masculine (*al-Baqarah* 2: 230, *al-Mujadilah* 58: 1) and the feminine (*al-Nisā'* 4: 20, *al-Baqarah* 2: 102)
3. Lamrabet prefers 'pairs' here to Asad's 'opposites' for *zawj* (Editor).
4. Translation by Muhammed Asad.

'partner' can be translated as either the man or the woman and sometimes, as is the case in this central verse, it remains totally abstract, apparently in order to better underline the Divine will to transcend gender when it comes to the first human design.

What's more, there is no Qur'anic affirmation which specifies that the Adam of this initial creation was male and even less that Eve was drawn from one of his ribs! Some Muslim scholars, both classical and contemporary, question and even refute this type of interpretation which seems to be, according to them, largely influenced by the previous scriptural texts.

These thinkers consider that the term 'Adam' is used primarily in the Qur'an in its broadest meaning of 'human being' or 'human kind'. In his various writings, the imam Muḥammad 'Abdu suggests that Adam also refers to individual, human being, 'al-insan' or 'bashar'. Adam, as he is mentioned in this verse, specifically seems to refer to 'humanity' in its entirety, which amounts to saying that in creating Adam, God created the human race, male and female at once, in its initial form.

This reading, which is dubbed *reformist* to distinguish it from *classical* approaches, advocates a single unique provenance for humanity, in other words a humanity which emerged from a single matter and same origin. Still within this reformist perspective, the objective of the verse describing creation would be to unequivocally affirm the original equality of all human beings. Unlike the classical reading which translates the term '*nafs*' by 'man' or 'Adam' and *zawj* by 'Eve' or 'the first woman', the term refers here and according to the perspective of these reformists, to 'the original essence', whereas '*zawj*' refers to 'partner', which supports the idea of a full human equality, beyond any considerations based on gender or race. Humanity was thus created from this 'first entity' or 'initial truth', and through his unique interpretation the definition by Imam Muhammad 'Abdu who, differs markedly from the classical commentators.

In fact imam 'Abdu has retained two quite similar versions of the term '*nafs wahida*'. One suggests that this initial entity refers to both sexes, male and female, which will subsequently evolve to produce the two partners and from there, all men and women. The other version considers that nothing in the Qur'an refutes the idea that this initial *'nafs'* is feminine, a view which is supported by the fact the term *'nafs'* itself is feminine and that the term *'zawj'* – masculine – implies husband since, in another verse, it is said:

> [...] so that man (zawjaha: 'her husband') might incline [with love] towards woman (nafs).[5] (al-A'rāf 7: 189)

Imam 'Abdu sees a justification of this reading in the titling of the surah, introduced by this verse, *'surah al-Nisā'* or 'The women'. This is a beautiful example of a feminine reading ....

It is clear that based on what some modern commentators have retained and without omitting the part of the occult or *'ghayb'* which characterizes any sacred text, one can suggest without taking too many risks that, in the Qur'anic version, human creation is not expressed through gender and that 'the Qur'an indiscriminately uses masculine and feminine words and images, in order to describe creation according to a single origin and substance. It is implicit in a great number of passages of the Qur'an that Allah's original creation was an undifferentiated humanity, neither man, nor woman'.

It seems, therefore, that God created man and woman simultaneously from a single substance and that these two human beings constitute the gender-based elements of a single, same reality. This corresponds precisely to this notion of *dualism* of creation, which is referred to several times in the Qur'an:[B]

> And in everything have We created opposites, so that you might bear in mind [that God alone is One]. (al-Dhāriyāt 51: 49)

In fact, man and woman as a 'pair' or 'couple' will confirm the central principle of the Qur'an: the creator is **One** whereas all of creation is in 'pairs'. And the term 'pairs' itself speaks to the notion of equality at all levels. This reformist reading of human creation seems to be the closest to the Qur'anic message which promotes

---

5. Translation by Muhammed Asad; parenthesis notes by Asma Lamrabet.

equality and human equity. One also notes that the entire story of the creation of humanity revolves around the central concept of Unicity or '*tawḥīd*', which is the very essence of Muslim spirituality.

Nonetheless, it is worth noting that a number of classical exegetes refer to certain hadiths, which refer to women in general, in order to *constrain* more or less the meaning of the text, in particular that concerning creation, and to extract a particular conception, namely that of a *subordinate* creation of women! This sadly leads to a religious justification of the structural inferiority of women.

Concerning the hadith taken as reference for the interpretation of the verse on creation, it seems there exists at least three versions, more or less similar, according to which the Prophet describes woman as '*created from a crooked rib which must not be forced at the risk of breaking it.*'[6]

The study of the Prophetic tradition suggests this hadith was formulated within the context of a set of recommendations relative to male-female relations and according to which the Prophet encouraged men to display kindness and softness towards women. The resemblance of these hadiths to the story of Adam and Eve in the biblical tradition encouraged scholars to draw parallels and conclude that Eve was brought forth from one of Adam's ribs. One notes in passing that the hadith in question nowhere refers to Adam. This interpretation is found traditionally in the majority of works of *tafasīr* despite the fact that, as we noted, nothing in the Qur'an affirms this concept.

One should not be surprised of this comparison undertaken between the tradition of the Prophet and the Judaeo-Christian myth because the hadith in question was elaborated in the context of a series of exhortations undertaken by the Prophet to his companions during the departing pilgrimage, where the topic itself was the recommendation to men to treat women well. The end of this hadith is the famous warning directed at believers: 'Be good towards your women.' The use of the imagery of the rib – and it is worth restating that the Prophet is not referring to Adam's rib – is in fact a metaphor, used according to an allegorical linguistic style

---

6. Hadith reported by Abu Hurayra in Sahih Bukhari and Sahih Muslim.

much appreciated by the Arabs of the time, in order to advise men to show sensitivity and kindness towards women. It is important to specify here that the said hadiths were not evoked by the Prophet in order to explain the biological aspect of human creation, as some contemporary [7] Muslim thinkers rightly point out, rather the objective was to challenge certain sexist traditions according to a very pedagogical strategy.

The Prophet, as was his habit, sought to inculcate in his companions the rules of propriety and consideration towards women and, thus, to soften the harsh norms of the era.

It is, therefore, obvious that any interpretation which draws from the hadiths in order to advance arguments in favour of the secondary creation of women and which attempts to diminish the status of women is necessarily erroneous and must be considered as being in opposition to the fundamental principles of the Qur'an and of the teachings of the Prophet.

This type of allegation, which is at the root of an entire universal heritage of the depreciation (discrediting?) of women, has long justified – and continues to do so in many cultures – a logic of oppression and humiliation of women.

A scholar as famous as Imam al-Razi believes that, in the following verse, can be found the evidence that women were created only in order to satisfy men's needs:

> *And among His wonders is this: He creates for you mates out of your own kind, so that you might incline towards them, and He engenders love and tenderness between you: in this, behold, there are signs indeed for people who think!* (al-Rūm 30: 21)

'There is proof in this verse that the creation of women is similar to that of animals, of plants and all other types of blessings[...] The creation of women is therefore a true blessing for us (men) and they have, therefore, essentially been created for us[...] This is explained through the fact that women are weak by their physical

---

7. Rachid al-Ghannoushi, *Al-Mar'a Bayna al-Qur'an wa Waqi' al-Muslimīn*, (London, Maghreb Center for Research and Translations, 2000), 15.

constitution, that they are foolish and puerile like children ... '[8]

If women were created by and for men, this confirms their structural inferiority and the requirement of their submissiveness. This type of assertion constitutes a recurring theme in all classical religious discourse and ends up outlining an ideological framework within which the subordination of women is incorporated into the language of the Sacred.

It is saddening to see the extent to which these scholars, who were negatively influenced by their socio-cultural environment and certain previous religious traditions, backed through their respective interpretations by an entire body of literature demeaning women and justifying the concept of male domination over women, in the name of Islam. From this, one understands how the vast majority of the religious arguments which legitimize the subordination of women draw their inspiration from this type of interpretation of Qur'anic verses, interpretations which with time are considered as somehow part of dogma, even confining the Qur'an itself to a secondary position.

It is well known that within other religious traditions, the indictment of the first woman, as being the one who led Adam – man – to be thrown out of Paradise, is obvious and this image of a temptress is undeniable. An entire legend full of imagery, with the forbidden tree, the snake and Eve, symbols of temptation and the fall from Eden, have been transmitted from generation to generation as being part of immutable religious concepts. None of these previous suppositions can be found in the Qur'an, not even in the form of a veiled reference.

Nonetheless, famous Muslim exegetes refer to these types of commentaries in their different works of *tafasīr*.[9] In fact, an exegete as famous as al-Qurṭubi states in his commentary that it was Eve who succumbed first to Satan and that it was she who led to the downfall of Adam, thus becoming the first source of temptation

---

8. Fakhr ar-Rāzī, *Tafsīr al-Kabīr, Mafatih al-Ghayb*, pp. 11–13.

9. Ibn Kathir says in his *Tafsīr* that a number of scholars which he refers to draw on ancient monotheistic sources ['*Isra'iliyaat*'] the story of the snake and of Satan, see p. 80.

for men![10]

Yet, nowhere in the Qur'an does it incriminate the first woman in humanity. The Qur'anic verses couldn't be clearer: It was the first human couple which was responsible and it has never been a question, according to revelation, of blaming one or the other.

> (*And We said: 'O Adam, dwell thou and thy wife in this garden, and eat freely thereof, both of you, whatever you may wish; but do not approach this one tree, lest you become wrongdoers.'*)
> *al-Baqarah* 2: 35

And it was both of them who succumbed to the temptation of Satan:

> (*But Satan caused them both to stumble therein, and thus brought about the loss of their erstwhile state. And so We said: 'Down with you, [and be henceforth] enemies unto one another; and on earth you shall have your abode and your livelihood for a while!'*)
> *al-Baqarah* 2: 36

Then the Qur'an describes how both of them, regretting their disobedience and dismayed at their fall from grace, implored God in order that He might forgive them.

That error, a symbol of the first act of human disobedience, was absolutely absolved by the Creator. It is one of the core concepts of Islam according to which the rehabilitation of human beings is total and entirely assumed by the Creator. There is no trace of the concept of the infamous original sin, weighing heavily on the whole of humanity, an irreparable error as it is described in the Christian tradition. According to the Islamic understanding, the forbidden tree is a symbol heavy with significance, designed to test this first couple of human beings, Adam and Eve. In the face of their clear-sightedness, their lucidity and their repentance, Allah forgives them ...

---

10. Al-Qurṭubi, *Al-Jami' li-Ahkam al-Qur'an*, Vol. I, p.408.

And from there, a sort of alliance between God and human beings was sealed via the intermediary of humanity's first couple ... No original sin but rather a sort of original pact between God and His creatures.[11]

That first erring has, therefore, not been written eternally into humanity's destiny as it has been transmitted in other religious traditions. God Says:

> And whatever [wrong] any human being commits rests upon himself alone [...] (al-An'ām 6: 164)

There is no notion of sin in the Christian sense of the term, nor eternal Divine punishment with its concepts of guilt, suffering or redemption.

The story of Adam and Eve, as it was interpreted in the biblical tradition and by extension in other religious traditions, is far removed from that advocated by the Qur'anic text.

In fact, in tracing the creation of these first human beings, the Qur'an depicts what could be referred to as the *first communal human experience* symbolized by these two first creatures. Firstly, God honoured the human being by referring to him as - '*khalifa*'[12] - on Earth or the 'legatee' of His knowledge. Then, Adam and Eve were raised to the ranks of 'learned beings', among those who 'know', in front of whom the angels – perfect beings – prostrated.

The angels prostrated in front of this human creature because God inculcated *knowledge* in him! Knowledge is at the root of creation ... Humans are above angels, despite the perfection of the latter, due to knowledge, reason and intelligence, qualities inherent to human beings.

The prostration of angels in front of human beings is the revelation of *humanism* in all its splendour as stated by the great Iranian thinker Ali Shariati![13]

---

11. Tariq Ramadan, *Les musulmans D'Occident et l'avenir de l'Islam*, (Paris: Sinbad-Actes Sud, 2003), p. 36.
12. The term *khalifa* is often translated as vicegerent or curator
13. Ali Shariati, 'Man's creation from the Islamic viewpoint'. See, http://www.shariati.com/english/human.html

These two beings created by God lived their first human trial in Paradise, when they infringed the Divine recommendation due to their weakness, their imperfection, in other words due to their humanity.

It was the first human experience of freedom ....

The first human uncertainty, the very first doubt, the first lesson in humility also ... despite their superiority in relation to the angels who prostrate before their knowledge, they are not infallible.

The Qur'an thus offers us a beautiful depiction of the human experience within the couple. Humanity's first couple will experience this first test in perfect communion. First man and first woman together, intimately connected, taken up the challenge of life ....

The Qur'an retraces in a harmonious fashion their fears and their joys, then their disobedience and their hopes, without ever distinguishing one from the other, and certainly not by denigrating one in relation to the other. Together they transgress and it is together that they repented. It is also together that they began a new destiny ....

A beautiful example of tribulations, patience, repentance and hope, whereby the return to God is always liberating.

A story of human experience which is both eternal and continuously renewed.

PART ONE

WHEN THE QUR'AN SPEAKS OF WOMEN

A story of all women
The Qur'anic text often cites, and at different points in the history of humanity, characters, *male or female*, with the constant objective of erecting them as living models for those who 'believe'.

These women and men are sometimes models of virtue to ponder upon and follow, sometimes models of vicissitude to recognize in order to know to avoid ... .

At times idealized characters, but never dehumanized, whom God cites all through His message not with the objective of distracting us but in order for us to extract a teaching, a route, a path to follow ... . .

Each woman and each man cited in the Qur'an have a singular history, a particular spiritual struggle, a different path, which distinguishes them from one another. God made things this way so that each of us, whoever we may be, can recognize ourselves one way or another, in their journey.

Their struggles, challenges, defeats or their victories are in a little way our own, if we know how to read them, if we know how to interpret them, how to translate them into the language of daily life.

Whatever the context, the location or the era, these beings chosen by God are signs all through the sacred book designed to remind us that we might advance in this life, slowly, patiently, inescapably towards His light ... . Adam, Nuh (Noah), Ibrahim (Abraham), Yusuf (Joseph), Musa (Moses), 'Isa (Jesus), Muhammad ... . But also Asiah, Sarah, Umm Musa, Maryam, *Balkis* ... . and so many others whose names were sometimes deliberately omitted because the example is not so much in the name as in the path and the moral conduct. It is also in the example set. And as believers, they are all, male and female, eternal models for us to return meaning to our history and our present ... .

God, through their respective tales, calls on our understanding, our reasoning and our capacity for discernment as human beings:

> *Indeed, in their stories [...] there is a lesson for those who are endowed with insight.*[1] (*Yusuf* 12: 111)

In addition, it is interesting to note that in the history of the great Prophets of humanity the particular presence, even crucial presence, of women as mothers in the paths and lives of these Prophets.

In fact, Isma'il (Ismael), Musa, 'Isa and Muhammad (peace be upon them) were all under the particular protection of their respective mothers, whereas history rarely reports a significant role for the father who is often absent or even inexistent, as in the story of 'Isa ... . .

These women who, in addition to their natural maternal role, have accompanied and protected God's emissaries on Earth. We, therefore, note throughout the history of these Prophets the pre-eminence of women – mothers – in the education, the protection and the diffusion of the Prophetic message. Women who have been veritable *intermediaries* of the sacred ... . .

And who would be surprised of this very feminine capacity to endure, resist and suffer all the contingencies of revelation? Their influence and involvement in the success of the transmission of the Divine message is evident and oft related in the sacred text.

But, far from enclosing women singularly in her natural – and no less important – role of *mother*, as many seem to do, the Qur'an

---

1. Here there is a slight difference from Asad's translation which mentions the story of 'these men'.

on the contrary outlines a variety of women's profiles, from the female governor represented by *Balkis*, to Zulaykha, the passionate woman, via the spiritual woman such as Maryam or the woman symbolising sacrifice, such as Asiah ... .

Ultimately, the Qur'anic vision refutes the traditional Muslim view which only recognizes and praises women as mothers first and foremost and which makes abstraction of her femininity.

In very many Islamic publications, women are only valued through their role as mothers, sisters or spouses. Never simply as *women* ... .

It is a concept which remains at *odds* with Islamic religious culture, despite the fact the Qur'an never ceases to underline the other dimensions of the feminine personality through the different representations of women cited in the text.

We too often forget that before being mothers, sisters or spouses, a woman is first and foremost a *woman* and that her *femininity* is an integral part of her personality as a human being.

Thus, through the different female characters described in the Qur'an, who transcend the share of humanity common with men, it is first and foremost the female side which is exalted through her abilities, her values, her abnegation, but also her faults and weaknesses ... .

And on this topic of female deficiencies, the Qur'an gives two examples which could be deemed pejorative, the remainder of the characters mentioned are in reality unquestionably positive models of womanhood. The two pejorative examples concern the spouses of Prophet Nuh (Noah) and Lut (Lot). This is how God describes them in His sacred Book:

> *For those who are bent on denying the truth God has propounded a parable in [the stories of] Noah's wife and Lot's wife: they were wedded to two of Our righteous servants, and each one betrayed her husband; and neither of the two [husbands] will be of any avail to these two women when they are told [on Judgment Day], "Enter the fire with all those [other sinners] who enter it!"* (al-Taḥrīm 66: 10)

It is interesting to note in this verse, that the *negative* aspect of these two women lies in their betrayal of their husbands as messengers of the Divine revelation. In fact, as Ibn 'Abbas clarifies in his exegesis,[2] it is not a question of a conjugal betrayal, but of a moral betrayal ... Various classical commentaries report that Noah's wife condemned her husband's spiritual activity to his enemies and used to mock his belief, branding him a madman, while the wife of Lut advocated sodomy and openly derided the moral values which he was trying to propagate among the people.

According to the majority of classical commentators, the critique which seems to be directed at them concerns their disloyal behaviour towards their partners.

The marital union which bound them implies respect of this alliance and thus a certain faithfulness, among others, to the spiritual undertakings of these two Prophets which the Qur'an refers to as *virtuous* men. They did not respect the message of justice and morality which these men, each according to their distinct path, sought to try and transmit to their respective peoples and worse, they denounced them to their enemies while denigrating their moral and spiritual aptitudes. It is here that resides any meaning to the condemnation of these women by the Creator ... The Qur'an here condemns the worse kind of betrayal, a moral betrayal which in addition places in peril the spread and viability of a message which was seeking to rehabilitate the utterly dissipated mores and customs of the time.

Aside from these two negative examples of women, the Qur'an *revives* the story of other women who each shone through a particular facet of their personality, while supporting their primordial role in the transformation of customs and traditions found throughout the history of humanity.

When the Qur'an speaks of women, it is all about love, beauty, intelligence and mercy which is read through words, signs and omissions ... yes, omissions, because one must know how to read not only what the Qur'an *says* clearly and what it *implies*, but also

2. *Tafsīr* Ibn 'Abbas, 'Surah *al-Taḥrīm*', p. 605, *Dar al-Kitab al-'Ilmiya*, Beirut, 2000.

what it omits ... An omission which can be very telling because it is symbolically very evocative ... .

Balkis, Queen of Sheba: A democratic queen

Whoever reads the Qur'an and stops on the verses of the Surah entitled 'The Ants' (*al-Naml*) might ask themselves why God gave the Queen of Sheba as an example. Historians have given her the name of *Balkis*[3] and assert that she reigned over the people of Sheba, the kingdom of which was in Yemen. The people of Sheba and their sovereign were known for their idolatry and history states that *Balkis* lived in a palace with three hundred and sixty windows in order to let the light of the sun through, before which she would prostrate every morning.[4]

Balkis one day received a message from the Prophet and no less King Solomon (*Solomon*) asking her to submit to the Creator of the world. What is interesting in this story told in the Qur'an is God's description of this woman. In fact, while the majority of kings and male governors referenced in the Qur'an are despots, as in the case of Pharaoh or Neron and others, the model of *Balkis*, female sovereign, is that of a monarch certainly, but a fair and enlightened monarch.

The depiction is of a female leader who was apparently very scrupulous concerning the political principles of equity and justice. The Qur'anic verses are in fact very explicit concerning the manner of governance of this illustrious woman. As soon as she receives the message from *Solomon*, she immediately convenes a council of dignitaries, conveys the content of the letter to them and asks them to reflect on the political decision which should be taken. This is what the Qur'an reports her as saying:

> *She added: 'O you nobles! Give me your opinion on the problem with which I am now faced; I would never make a [weighty] decision unless you are present with me. (al-Naml 27: 32)*

3. Nowhere does the Qur'an mention the name *Balkis*.
4. Muhammed Chiadmi *The Noble Qur'an, a new French translation of the meaning of these verses,* , Tawhid (Lyon: Editions, 2004), notes from the bottom of the page of Surah 27, verse 23.

A female leader of one of the richest kingdoms of the era and who makes the effort to consult the elected representatives of her people! The latter inform her that the final decision rested with her alone, but that she could rely on their physical and material strength:

> They answered: "We are endowed with power and with mighty prowess in war - but the command is thine; consider, then, what thou wouldst command". (al-Naml 27: 33)

The famous exegete al-Zamakhshari[5] explains in his commentary that the representatives consulted by *Balkis*, while leaving the ultimate decision with her, undertook a demonstration of their force and power, suggesting they would rather be in favour of bellicose action. However, *Balkis* did not agree with this approach, since she suggested a peaceful solution as a first response, namely the act of sending *Solomon* a gift with the objective of testing his reaction.

This pondered political decision reflects the great wisdom of this queen, who in passing, also made a pertinent remark on the despotism of kings ... An intriguing comment, considering she herself was a queen, but one can also read therein her concern to avoid precisely the type of corruption typically associated with autocratic power.

> (*Said she: 'Verily, whenever kings enter a country they corrupt it, and turn the noblest of its people into the most abject. And this is the way they [always] behave? Hence, behold, I am going to send a gift to those [people], and await whatever [answer] the envoys bring back.'*) al-Naml 27: 34–35

An attentive reading of these verses indicates the extent to which the observations of this queen are politically grounded. The political message which she sought to transmit here could not be clearer. It represents an acerbic critique of all forms of despotism which

---

5. Al-Zamakhshari, *Al-Kashshaf*, ch. 3, p. 375.

can be found recurrently in the history of humanity with their corollaries of humiliation and oppression experienced by peoples who, as she says so well, go so far as to 'lose their *human dignity*' under the governance of authoritarian political powers.

What is more, her political analysis is of great relevance for those observers of the disastrous management of politics in Muslim lands and enlightens us, where needed, on the necessity of justice and fairness in the Qur'anic message. A requirement which constitutes the cornerstone of the Islamic moral and legal system. Ibn 'Abbas, the famous and first Muslim exegete, nicknamed the 'Interpreter of the Qur'an' or,'*Turjuman al-Qur'an*' attributes the following verse '*This is the manner in which they usual behave*' to God Himself, responding to *Balkis*' commentary and confirming her earlier analysis on dictatorial political systems. What more telling testimony than this one could we need to illustrate the judgement and political perspicacity of this woman?!

Thus, *Balkis* demonstrated political wisdom but also intelligence, because in sending the present to Solomon, she was judiciously disregarding the rash proposition of her advisers in order to avoid an unnecessary war and, by the same token, she was buying time to reflect in order to study the personality of this king.

Balkis wanted to test *Solomon* and see what was behind this message in which he was exhorting her to submit to the *One God*. If the king accepted her present, it would mean his mission reflected earthly ambitions, however, any refusal would suggest *Solomon*'s motivation was more profound, in other words, of a spiritual order ... A veritable diplomatic strategy!

Sayyid Qutb perceives, through the character of this Queen, the essence of woman in all her femininity, the woman who through her instinct and her innate female intuition refuses wars and conflict and prefers peace and dialogue.[6] Is it not said that women embody

---

6. Sayyid Qutb, *Fi- Zilal al-Qur'an*, Surah *al-Naml*. It is necessary to state that this female intuition is not always obvious and that the female model is not necessarily a model of peace and gentleness? This is the case of the woman nicknamed 'the Iron Lady' Margaret Thatcher, PM, who led Britain into the 'Falklands War' in 1982. Or, more recently that of the American Secretary of State, Condolezza Rice, very much in favour of 'pre-emptive wars'!

a part, however minute, of the infinite mercy or *Rahma* of God on earth? This quality which some interpret as a sign of weakness in women, is on the contrary symbolized in the Qur'an as a sign of intelligence and great moral force in this woman queen. A sovereign who reigns politically, with reason and wisdom, while maintaining her woman's humanity as a gift from God. It is as though in some ways, she humanizes her political action through her feminine sensibility which makes her closer to the daily human realities.

The description which the Qur'an makes of this woman *head of state* is in and of itself an undeniable refutation of all the allegations of the hyper-emotionalism of women who are said to reason-less well than men due to the *hyperemotivity* of their personality and who, according to the same logic, cannot lead, politically speaking, an entire people! This is the explanation found in the discourse of almost all the Muslim scholars, and this regardless of the era.

Women are said to be very sensitive, excessively sentimental and therefore vulnerable, emotionally speaking, which renders her incapable of using her reason, and in the management of state affairs; there is no room for feelings or emotions reason rules.

However, putting forth arguments which suggest that women reason less or that their ability to reason is subject to her emotions is equivalent to saying that she is less human. In fact, if we were to distinguish human beings from the other terrestrial creatures, one would note that it is indeed reason, this essentially human ability, which differentiates us from the rest of Divine creation and which allows us to accede to this privileged dimension of human beings through our faculties of reason and discernment.

In assuming that women have deficiencies in this area, they are being deprived quite simply of a part of their reason and, therefore, of their humanity.

In Islamic literature, validating these sorts of theses from the religious standpoint has always been an easy task given the anchoring of such traditions in the popular imagination which stipulates the supremacy of man regardless of the context or social environment. Concerning political affairs and governance, given the assumption that man is stronger, less emotional and, therefore, more reasonable, he is definitively viewed as more apt than women at managing these sorts of situations. Nonetheless, it is worth noting that these sorts of macho assumptions are not specific to Muslim peoples alone, far from it. They can be found in all societies, even in those considered most advanced. In France for example,[7] the land of human rights and the cradle of *feminism*, the parliament is composed of 89% men and women's struggle for political equality still has a long way to go.

Nonetheless, it remains true that in our Muslim context, women's access to positions of political responsibility is often, if not always, forbidden in the name of Islam ... And it is just as surprising to see how the so-called ban on women acceding to the highest spheres of political governance is Islamically justified through a single hadith – only one – which has become the norm, if not the sword of Damocles brandished over heads each time the issue of women's political participation is raised in the lands of Islam.

There does indeed exist a saying from the Prophetic tradition which states: 'A nation cannot succeed if it is led by a woman or if it leaves political power in the hands of a woman ...'.[8]

On the other hand, one must underline that the context in which this hadith was formulated has often been ignored, which significantly restricts the account of its true significance ... In fact, it occurred when the Prophet had learned that Chosroes II, Emperor of Persia and inveterate enemy of the Muslims, had died and that his daughter had taken over leadership in his place ... The Persian empire of the time was governed with a hand of steel by the ruling family which was known for its insidious despotism. The Prophet was seeking through this phrase to denigrate the daughter of the emperor due to the state of war which prevailed between the two peoples and due also to the politically autocratic regime which

7. Website for the French parliament: 502 men and 75 women in 2006. For more on this topic see: Regine Saint Criq and Nathalie Prevost, *Vol au-dessus d'un nid de machos*, which outlines the struggles faced by women on the French political scene.
8. Hadith transmitted by Abu Bakrah, reported by Bukhari, Tirmidhi, Nasa'i and Aḥmad, not reported by Muslim.

lived there and not, to criticize the fact she was a woman. We can at this level pose the question differently: would the Prophet have glorified the ascension to power of the Persian Empire if it had been the son and not the daughter of Chosroes II who had succeeded him? Evidently not. The Prophet criticized the nature of power and the entire political system of the Persian empire of the time! Yet, it is sad to note that a certain, profoundly misogynistic religious reading perceived, through this hadith, the absolute need to impose the nomination of a man for all positions of political responsibility.

It is interesting to note that Abu Bakrah,[9] narrator of the hadith, *recalled* this particular hadith for the first time in a historical context as particular as that in which it was uttered by the Prophet!

Indeed, the story of the tradition states that Abu Bakrah recalled this hadith during the famous 'Battle of the Camel' in which were confronted the allies of A'ishah and those of Ali ibn Abu Talib.[10] Abu Bakrah, himself an ally of A'ishah's clan, justified his own refusal to participate in the battle on the basis that it was A'ishah, a woman, who was leading the political action! Abu Bakrah thus made the link between the hadith he had heard from the Prophet and the context of conflict which opposed A'ishah to Imam Ali and which sadly turned to tragedy.

Having interpreted the hadith literally, he considered illicit any participation in an activity led by a woman even if, in this case, it was A'ishah who he held in very high esteem according to certain Islamic sources.[11]

It is important to note in this regard and concerning this political episode, that the justification given by Abu Bakrah was not repeated by any of the great companions of the Prophet at the time, who themselves abstained from participating in the battle of the camel based on other considerations.

Whereas the Prophet criticized a political framework due to its

---

9. Of his real name, Nafi' ibn al-Harith, he was nicknamed 'Abu Bakrah after his conversion to Islam.

10. See the details of this battle in our essay: '*Âïsha épouse du Prophèt ou l'Islam au féminin*', (Lyon: Editions Tawhid, 2004).

11. See all the commentaries concerning Abu Bakrah in the collection of al-Haytami, *Majma'a Azawa'id wa Manba' al-Fawâ'id*, vol. v., p. 209.

authoritarianism, Abu Bakrah understood this to mean – as many of the scholars after him did – that it was all political representation of women which should be forbidden.

The following generation of scholars ended up inserting this hadith into the register of recommendations in favour of the prohibition of all political participation by women despite, the fact the Prophet never enjoined anything on the subject. He was merely making an observation of the Persian political situation of the time, and any instrumentalization of this hadith has been undertaken in defiance of the context in which it was formulated and with the intended objective of denying women any form of political participation.[12]

What's more, some thinkers, notably contemporary ones, affirm that this hadith, being a simple *ahad hadith* (hadith reported by a single narrator), cannot logically, therefore, be used as a single source of legislation.[13]

The interpretation of this hadith has had the most widespread impact we know, with the corollary of *justifications*, the most in vogue of which remain the notion of the *structural weakness* of women. The scholars banned women from having access to all political responsibility due to this alleged structural weakness, which puts them in a state of moral and intellectual incapacity to manage the affairs of the State! Women are said to be *weaker* due to their physical constitution and their biological propensity to conceive of everything on an emotional level, which is said to render them predominantly *irrational*. What is being confused here are emotional predispositions and intellectual capabilities. Yet, there is a big difference between saying that women have a greater inclination towards sensitivity and affectivity – which in no way represents a weakness – and suggesting they are somehow handicapped by this! Is the suggestion that a female neurosurgeon

---

12. For further details, see: Fatima Mernissi, *Le harem politique, Le Prophète et les femmes*, chap. 'Enquête sur un hadith misogyne et sur son auteur Abu Bakrah', (Paris: Albin Michel, 1987.)
13. Heba Raouf Ezzat, 'Women and the interpretation of Islamic sources', *Islamic Research Foundation International, Inc.* [www.irfi.org]. <http://www.irfi. org/articles/articles_451_500/women_and_the_interpretation_of.htm>

who operates each morning in order to extract cerebral tumours from men is incapable of controlling her alleged over-emotionalism in the political sphere, when she clearly does so without issue on the operating table?

All these affirmations, in addition to being erroneous and unjustified, are in flagrant contradiction with Qur'anic principles. The Qur'an has never advocated any sort of weakness which is singular to women and nowhere does it stipulate that man is endowed with greater reason or that women are more deficient than men or that women are devoid of rationality. Nowhere ... ! However the Qur'an has stated that *human beings* in general are *weak*:

man has been created weak. [...] (al-Nisā' 4: 28)

The weakness referred to by the Qur'an here is a deficiency linked to the creation of human beings themselves, due to their incapacity to control their negative impulses, a weakness intrinsic to human beings and which transcends gender.

What is more, through the example of *Balkis*, the Qur'an counters all the presumptions which tend to paint women as inferior and exclude her, politically speaking, by raising a woman to the height of wisdom, as a democratic political leader, fair and capable ... Infinitely wiser than all of those men she consulted and who appear to be the dignitaries of her people. And, yet, it is deplorable to see how certain classical Muslim commentators have strongly criticized the person of *Balkis*. Whereas the Qur'an speaks of her in glowing, respectful terms which could not be clearer nor more precise, many exegetes have a pernicious approach to this individual and a number of them get mired in very long, harsh and often very disagreeable commentaries!

Whosoever reads the various works of exegesis will recall the awkwardness, the reticence, even the hostility of certain exegetes faced with a female personality reigning on a *magnificent throne*[14] and who in addition, displayed intelligence and wisdom! It is worth

---

14. '*Wa-laha 'arsh 'azim*': 'she has a magnificent throne', such is the Qur'an's description.

noting here that the Qur'an describes the throne, emblem of her power, as magnificent, suggesting a significant intellectual capacity of this woman who managed this vast and rich kingdom with such know-how!

Some erudite Muslims avoid the crux of the matter, namely the extraordinary personality of this queen as described in the Qur'an, as well as her political capabilities, in favour of a very reductive approach which sometimes veers into deeply disparaging. This is the case of a famous theologian of the early period of Islam who describes her as a '*iljatu*', a pejorative term which means 'donkey' or 'disbeliever', an expression often used to refer disparagingly, even insultingly to non-believers. This scholar expresses surprise at seeing men allowing themselves to be governed by an '*iljatu*' who, being a woman is deemed weak and lacking in reason but who turns out to be, much to his disappointment, more intelligent than the men – said to be sages – who surrounded her! They push their derision to the point of inappropriately criticising her physique.[15] One might ask what the link is between this woman's physical appearance and her political decisions, her physical appearance having been born of Divine creation! And how can he vilify and belittle her entire person simply because she happens to be a woman?!

Other scholars go further and even suggest this poor queen has *jinn* ancestry! *Balkis'* mother must be a *jinn*, and according to some even the leader of *jinns*![16] It is only by diminishing her humanity that the commentators can rest assured concerning her future as a woman ... no need to take her as an example if she is really only half human! In reading the commentary attributed to the story of *Balkis*, one is stunned in the face of so much speculation and unlikely stories which turn the reader away from the true educational dimension of this story.

At the end of his commentary on these verses, Ibn Kathir almost apologizes for having had to report so many legends and

---

15. *Tafsīr* Ibn Kathir, Beirut: *Dar al-Kutub al-Ilmyya*, 2007, p. 339. The scholar in question is Hasan al-Basri, cited by Ibn Kathir.
16. *Tafsīr* Ibn Kathir, reported by Qatadah, Zuhayr ibn Muhammad as well as in the Qur'anic commentary of al-Qurṭubi.

mischievous tales concerning *Balkis*. He recognizes the improbable nature of a great number of the stories and inappropriate interpretations which run counter to the deference and the sobriety of the Qur'anic description.[17]

One is within one's rights to ask questions and to query why this denigration occurs when God Himself in His Qur'an mentions *Balkis* in very respectful terms and with an extreme sensitivity. In fact, one notes that even in terms of her idolatry, God does not refer to her as a miscreant or impious but, rather, He depicts her as having been forced to submit to the religious culture of her people and was – somewhat despite herself – from a disbelieving people:

> [*And she has recognized the truth] although that which she has been wont to worship instead of God had kept her away [from the right path]: for, behold, she is descended of people who deny the truth!' (al-Naml* 27: 43)

In re-reading these verses concerning *Balkis* attentively, one is surprised by the enormous discord between the Qur'anic verses, full of regard for her person and the inconceivable interpretations which one finds in the classical books of exegesis. God, in His sacred Qur'an has never ceased to *highlight* the image of this woman, queen, non-believer, sage, defender of the values of Justice. One perceives, through the portrait painted by the sacred text and all along the Divine narration, the emotional and spiritual aptitude of this woman who ultimately was very sensitive to the message of Prophet *Solomon*. She must surely have discerned in this message the signs of this Truth which she had always sought from the depths of her soul ... God wanted to deliberately embellish the image of this non-believing woman in order that we might better appreciate her once she had converted to the faith of the One God!

As it happens, the Qur'anic message couldn't be clearer concerning the importance given to the consultation of governed peoples and to the values of ethics and justice which the government must reflect. *Balkis*, queen and woman, has perfectly symbolized this

---

17. See the end of the commentary of Ibn Kathir in his *Tafsīr*.

profile of a head of state at the extreme opposite of despotic power, which the Qur'an never ceases to reject throughout its message. Moreover, one might note that in the Qur'an, these authoritarian powers are almost always symbolized by male dictators! It even appears that she is the only political personality endowed with such authority and who was elevated as an *ideal*, strictly speaking, in the Holy Qur'an. Thus, she is an example of political management for all, men and women. It is also interesting to highlight the strong personality of this woman who, once convinced of the sincerity of *Solomon* and the veracity of his message, solemnly announced her submission to the Creator with much humility but also great dignity. In fact, the Qur'an reports her words as follows:

> *Cried she: 'O my Sustainer! I have been sinning against myself thy worshipping aught but Thee: but [now] I have surrendered myself, with Solomon, unto the Sustainer of all the worlds!' (al-Naml 27: 44)*

It is with *Solomon* – and not for him – that she submits to the Lord of the universe! With him! A manner in which devotion to God is undertaken in the most spontaneous *equality* and the deepest *freedom* ... Of course she was amazed by the supernatural powers of king Solomon and by his surprising abilities but she was conscious that all of his abilities were God given and that rather it was the Prophet and his spiritual message which had won his heart ... . The story states that *Solomon* and *Balkis* married,[18] though nothing can confirm this fact. Nonetheless, we would like to believe it! No surpris here if these two beings have admiration for one another! Were they not both enamoured by the values of justice and probity? Was it not submission to the Creator of the world which brought them together? It is a beautiful story of love and understanding which the Qur'an offers us here through this female character, a character which has little to do with what a number of exegetes have sadly reported.

---

18. A controversial view, Tabari claims that *Solomon* rather married her to a notable.

Sarah and Hagar, emblems of monotheism

Sarah and Hagar represent without doubt the two female ancestors of monotheism.

Sarah, mother of Ishaq (Isaac) and Hagar, mother of Isma'il ... Ishaq and Isma'il, two Prophets from the same father, Ibrahim and from whom the ineluctable separation will happen between two peoples who until today will live in perpetual confrontation ... .

Prophet Ibrahim had as his first wife Sarah. All the monotheistic traditions agree on the fact she was a woman of extreme beauty. The Prophet described her as the most beautiful woman of humanity after Eve.[19] Sarah and Ibrahim after many years of marriage were unable to have children. Abraham never complained but Sarah, through that specifically feminine perception, painfully felt, in the depths of her heart, the disavowed desire of her husband to have a child.

This is how, in conformity with the customs of the time which attributed sterility first and foremost to women – a custom which persists to this day – she offered her servant Hagar, brought from Egypt, to her beloved husband. Feeling guilty because of this sterility which she had to take upon herself alone, she thought to remedy this *fault* by *offering* him, with death in her soul, her young Egyptian servant.

Some time after, Sarah received news which would turn the rest of her life upside down and transform the destiny of humanity ... She was with child! The Qur'an cites Sarah in the following verses describing her joy and happiness at the announcement by the angels of her future pregnancy:

> AND, INDEED, there came unto Abraham Our [heavenly] messengers, bearing a glad tiding. They bade him peace; [and] he answered, '[And upon you be] peace!'-and made haste to place before them a roasted calf. But when he saw that their hands did not reach out towards it, he deemed their conduct strange and became apprehensive of them. [But]

---

19. Commentary on historical facts are drawn from the work *Nisa' khalidat* by Dr Tareq al-Suwaidan."

they said: "Fear not! Behold, we are sent to the people of Lot."
And his wife, standing [nearby], laughed [with happiness];
whereupon We gave her the glad tiding of [the birth of] Isaac
and, after Isaac, of [his son] Jacob. Said she: "Oh, woe is
me! Shall I bear a child, now that I am an old woman and
this husband of mine is an old man? Verily, that would be a
strange thing indeed!" Dost thou deem it strange that God
should decree what He wills? The grace of God and His
blessings be upon you, O people of this house! Verily, ever to
be praised, sublime is He! (*Hūd* 11: 69–73)

Through these verses, one notes that Sarah is present by the side of
her husband as he receives apparently foreign guests. These guests
were in fact emissaries of God, in other words, angels in human
form and who in all likelihood deeply unsettled Ibrahim and his
spouse due to their refusal to taste the roasted veal they were
offering. The messengers sought initially to reassure their hosts by
informing them that they were sent by God to the people of Lut,
and subsequently, they announced to Sarah the news of her future
descendants. She who was already at such an advanced stage of her
life, and who had always considered herself to be sterile, and who in
addition had as a husband, a man as elderly as Ibrahim, struggled
to believe the news!

Faced with her surprise, the angels reminded her that nothing
can stand in the way of God's Will and that He is the one through
which everything, absolutely everything becomes possible. There is
in fact a real dialogue happening between Sarah and the angels,
messengers of God, which is testimony to the rank of this woman in
the eyes of God. Sarah, the wife of Ibrahim and constant companion
shared with him the heavy weight of this message of faith and
belief. They were both partners in the intimacy of conjugal life and
in the intimacy of the proximity to God. The explicit reference to
Sarah in this verse, mentioned under the designation of the wife of
Ibrahim and the blessing of the angels on both of them confirms
the spiritual intimacy of these two beings: *'The grace of God and His*
blessings be upon you, O people of this house!' God blesses Sarah and

Ibrahim by granting them this noble lineage of Prophets Ishaq and Yaqub.

God blesses them both and grants them His gifts and His infinite mercy ... Sarah was there, present by the side of Ibrahim, first as his wife, partner of this illustrious patriarch, his wife in the good and bad times and finally after a very long life together, as a mother, when she had *offered* him another woman in a moment of despair, in order to permit him to have a lineage. God rewards them with filiations just for them ... .

God gifted Sarah the much wanted child that she despaired of having one day, and through this child, granted her the permanence of her name through a long and noble lineage made up of Prophets and messengers.

Meanwhile Hagar, the servant offered by Sarah to her husband, had already given birth to Isma'il and Ibrahim received the Divine order to emigrate with his new family from Jerusalem to Makkah, still uninhabited at the time, and to return straight after to Jerusalem ... Ibrahim spoke of this Divine order to no one, not even to Hagar who was accompanying him.

Torment gnawed at his heart at the thought of having to abandon these two beings without any protection in this foreign land, but the Divine injunction was clear and no doubt it was his trust in God's mercy which gave him the strength to continue. Once they'd arrived at their destination, Ibrahim, stricken by sadness, somehow abandoned Hagar and her son, still then an infant, without being able to give them any explanation and headed back on the return journey. That was what God had ordered of him and Ibrahim, *al-Hanif* ('primordial monotheist'), known for his moral rectitude, could only obey. The tradition states that Hagar was initially distraught at finding herself alone in this arid and desert region and, seeing Ibrahim leave without saying a word, she called out to him several times: 'Are you going to leave us here, me and your son, alone in this forgotten place?' Ibrahim, apparently torn between his submission to God and his love for his family did not dare turn around and risk faltering and succumbing to the temptation of taking them back with him. Hagar, still unable to believe what was happening to her, continued to follow him, with her baby in her arms and asking him the same question: 'Are you going to leave us here alone?'

Faced with the silence of her spouse, she began to perceive in the depth of her heart that what she was experiencing was not fortuitous and that something very important was underway in the silence of this place. It was as if time had stopped, as Ibrahim through his muteness, his disarray but also the strength of his conviction, had transmitted the breath of the Divine message to her.

Ibrahim's decision to leave them alone did not emanate from him! He must be obeying an order which superseded him as a human, she told herself. She had a deep premonition in the depths of her being ... .

She then asked him a question which speaks volumes on her spiritual state of being: *'Was it God who ordered you to abandon me and this poor child in this place?'* '*Yes*', admitted Ibrahim, his throat tight with emotion, while continuing his route and while still unable to return to her. Her premonition was confirmed. It was an order from the Creator.

'So certainly God will not abandon us!' she answered in response. A response laden with meaning, with serenity and emotion ... it is as if somehow she felt appeased. If God decided it, the rest is irrelevant! How many times have we been confronted with difficult circumstances in our lives, with acts and decisions which are beyond our control as human beings? But once convinced by the strength of destiny and once we place our trust in God, a pleasurable feeling of relief and appeasement comes over us without our problems necessarily being resolved! It is this subtle and beautiful serenity which only faith can awaken in the depth of our souls, which allows us to resist so many struggles, so much sadness and so much pain in our lives ... .

Hagar lived as a believer, she was confident; if such is the will of God, then she would submit to it willingly. Here is an example which could not be more telling of true submission to the Creator. She stopped at the edge of a valley and tried to cling to this hope, that little voice deep within which was telling her that no evil could touch her if such was the decision of the Master of the Universes. He was her sole Protector ... . At the same moment, Ibrahim, on his journey home, was calling on God, imploring Him to protect his family:

> O our Sustainer! Behold, I have settled some of my offspring in a valley in which there is no arable land, close to Thy sanctified Temple, so that, O our Sustainer, they might devote themselves to prayer: cause Thou, therefore, people's hearts to incline towards them and grant them fruitful sustenance, so that they might have cause to be grateful. (Ibrahim 14: 37)

Hagar, once Ibrahim had disappeared from the horizon, kept repeating this phrase, which in addition to giving her strength was doing her so much good: 'He won't abandon us' Those who follow God's path cannot have fear ... .

Certainly, her faith comforted her, but she was a poor mother who, despite her profound trust in God, was scared for her little loved one, all the more given that he began crying inconsolably. He was crying from thirst and hunger, when all around them there was utter desolation and sadness ... How to receive help in this uninhabited valley? How and where to find water in this desolate region? Distraught and terrified, faced with the incessant cries of her little one, she placed him on the edge of the valley, seeking desperately here and there, a tree, a sign or a living soul.

Not knowing where to go in order to find help, she undertook to walk alternately between Mount Safa and Mount Marwa. She thus found herself walking and running, several times, between these two mounts while scrutinizing the horizon and hoping to identify help from the side of Safa, or listening intently for a noise or familiar sound from the side of Marwa!

After seven back and forth journeys between the two mounts, she threw herself to the ground, exhausted, bemoaning with her whole being her powerlessness and suffering. How great must have been her anguish at seeing her son suffering without being able to assist him in any way! She hid her face in order to no longer see her child perishing before her eyes ... She would have preferred in that instant to have been buried herself than to live this! Suddenly in the middle of the terrifying silence which reigned in that place and which was broken only by the sobs and cries of her baby, she noticed a limpid and clear water beneath the fingers of her child! Wild with joy and happiness, she ran to the source to quench her son's thirst and while drinking herself she tried to hold on to the stream of water with her hands while saying: 'Zam ... Zam ... ', a term which in Arabic means 'to hold tightly' and which translates her fear of seeing that water source disappear as abruptly as it had appeared.

Some texts from within the tradition report that it is the archangel Gabriel (*Jibril*) who planted the water source under the fingers of Isma'il, when others relate the material manifestation of the archangel, who spoke to Hagar and indicated to her the location of the water source.[20]

This episode in the story of Hagar is here to remind us of the profound meaning of two events of extreme importance for Islam and Muslims: the ritual of *as-Sa'i* or the seven back and forth runs between Safa and Marwa during the hajj or pilgrimage, and the symbolism of the water source of Zamzam which from that day is still present in the Holy land of Makkah ... .

As-Sa'i, which symbolizes therefore the back and forth, is an Arabic expression which means, 'relentlessness' or 'ardour' in the pursuit of an objective. During the pilgrimage, one makes the 'effort' to undertake the journey between Safa and Marwa exactly as Hagar did to rescue her thirsty child.

After the advent of Islam, the Qur'an renewed the story of Hagar and God wanted, through the prescription of this ritual of the seven back and forth runs between the two mounts of Safa and Marwa, to remind us that it was her, Hagar, whom we remember and her alone ... .

This ritual remains one of the central moments of the annual Muslim pilgrimage and the hajj is invalid without its undertaking. For over fourteen centuries, millions of Muslims walk and run, every year, between the two mounts following in Hagar's footsteps!

20. Tabari, *Tarikh al-Umam wal-Muluk*, (Beirut: Dar Sader, 2003, p. 84–85).

Could we possibly imagine rendering a greater tribute to a human being than to celebrate their memory in this fashion? The story of the commemoration of a woman in Islam ... Islam, which is often accused of humiliating women, eternally glorifies the memory of a woman by inscribing her path as one of the pillars of the worship of God!

> *[Hence,] behold, As-Safa and Al-Marwah are among the symbols set up by God [...]* (al-Baqarah 2: 158)

Certainly, it should be noted that Hagar is never mentioned by the Qur'anic text, except for an allusion during the invocation by Ibrahim and found in the following verse: '*Oh our Lord, I have installed a group of my descendants in a valley without culture, near Your sacred oratory – the Ka'ba [...].*' It is the tradition of the Prophet and the entirety of the corpus of exegesis which will recall the story of Hagar. Nonetheless, though she might seem absent, not least through a specific reference in the Qur'anic text, her memory is reprised in a formal way in dogma and in the ritual of Islam. Without naming her, the ritual of Safa and Marwa during the pilgrimage remains the indelible testimony of her journey, of her distress, of her presence.

It is therefore an example which honours *women*, which commemorates for eternity their patience, their devotion and sacrifice. Pilgrims from all times and all places celebrate the memory of Hagar each year and, in completing this pillar of Islam, they will celebrate the memory of a woman who submitted to the commandments of her creator in the most profound act of abnegation.

How many of them today recall the story of this woman during their pilgrimage? Are they conscious that it is in His name and for God that this ritual was revived in Islam? Do they understand that it is in memory of a woman that they solemnly celebrate this ritual? A woman whom the Prophet himself also respectfully evoked in a hadith: '*If you arrive in Egypt, I recommend you treat its inhabitants well and wish them well because there is between them and us an alliance of protection and kinship.*' The kinship of which the Prophet speaks is that of Hagar.[21]

And what shall we say of this water source of Zamzam which was granted to her through the grace of God to quench her son Isma'il? This water, which the Prophet Muhammad never ceased to praise in numerous hadiths the benefits of, and which all pilgrims are meant to drink upon their arrival in the holy land. This inexhaustible source of water illustrates the generosity of God towards this arid land, as well as the Divine reward gifted to this exemplary believer.

It is important to underline the symbolism of this water since the Sunnah reminds us that it was the grandfather of the Prophet, 'Abd al-Muṭṭalib, who will rediscover the wells of Zamzam some time before the birth of the Messenger of Islam, an event which confirms the continuity established between the two Prophets Isma'il and Muhammad, peace be upon them.

The tradition is silent after the events experienced by Hagar and her son Isma'il, whom we will rediscover later with his father Ibrahim during the construction of the Kaaba.

Isma'il, raised by this mother, the emblem of devotion, who himself will manifest this same sublime abnegation to God during the story of the offering and the sacrifice. The gift of the Self of Ibrahim, of Sarah, of Hagar and of her son Isma'il ... .

A story of sacrifices, of all the sacrifices, where all these beings were chosen by God to become veritable symbols of devotion to the Creator. Re-reading their story is to remind ourselves continuously of the true meaning of submission to God, the first pillar of Islam. To always be with God and to submit to His Truth no matter the difficulty, the test or the suffering ... and whatever the sacrifice may cost us!

Sarah, the lady of the house and free woman, and Hagar, abandoned and humble servant, are equal before God. They both received the same Divine favour, the same gifts, the same sublime honour of being women whose name will forever transcend the memory of humanity.

---

21. Tabari, *Tarikh*, vol. 1, p. 82.

Zulaykha, or forbidden love

Zulaykha is a female character who seems to have a negative role in the story of Prophet Yusuf, and this, as much in a given body of Islamic literature as in the Judaeo-Christian tradition, where she does not appear to have been spared either since she symbolizes the perverse character of the ultimate *temptress*.

The Qur'an, as is custom, does not mention her name and refers to her discreetly as *imra'at al-'Aziz*, in other words, the 'wife of al-'Aziz'. The ancient historians and Muslim scholars diverge as to her real name, some such as Tabari, Ibn Ishaq and Ibn Abbas refer to her as Rael, whereas for others, she is Zulaykha.[22]

The story of Prophet Yusuf is the only one in the Qur'an which is related in its entirety and in an exhaustive manner within a same surah, specifically surah *Yūsuf*. From the beginning to the end, the story keeps us in suspense and subjugates us through its allegories laden with meaning, with beauty and with truth, like a pure spring.

It is one of these Qur'anic stories rich in teachings, in morals, in the ethics of life and where the Divine pedagogy tells us one of its most beautiful stories. This is how the Qur'an itself describes and begins the story of Yusuf:

> *In the measure that We reveal this Qur'an unto thee,*
> *[O Prophet,] We explain it to thee in the best possible way,*
> *seeing that ere this thou wert indeed among those who are*
> *unaware [of what revelation is]. (Yūsuf 12: 3)*

It is true that the story of this messenger is very beautiful.

Yusuf[23] is the inheritor of a noble lineage of Prophets, since he is the grandson of Ishaq, himself the son of Ibrahim. Since he was a child, he was destined to have an extraordinary future. He was the favourite out of twelve siblings, enlightened, intelligent and apparently gifted with a particular ability for the interpretation of dreams and moreover, extremely handsome! The Prophet

---

22. *Tafsīr* Ibn Kathir, p. 448.
23. The whole story which follows is drawn from the work of the historian Tabari in his *Tarikh*, p. 111.

Muhammad refers in one of his hadiths to the great physical beauty of this Messenger of God.[24]

The Chronology of events, as it is announced in the Qur'an, teaches us that Yusuf, his father's favourite, favoured through his great beauty but also by his great wisdom and his particular ability as an oracle, was the victim of a sick jealousy from among his own brothers who sought to assassinate him.

He was however saved at the last minute and sold into slavery to one of the nobles of the time, al-'Aziz known as Potiphar in the ancient monotheistic scriptures. As is underlined by Tabari, al-'Aziz as it is mentioned in the Qur'an, is a title of nobility and does not correspond to the first name of the person, whom the Qur'an also remains silent about.

Yusuf was thus adopted by the family of this rich individual. As he was intelligent and hard-working, he moved up from his position of humble teenage slave to managing the internal affairs of the couple with whom he was living.

Zulaykha, wife of al-'Aziz, who is also described in the tradition as beautiful and wealthy, fell in love with this young and magnificent slave who lived in her home and with whom she rubbed shoulders on a daily basis.

It is true that Yusuf presented a major disadvantage in Egyptian society of the time, reputed for its lax mores: he was too handsome! The Qur'anic text describes the scene of the infamous temptation very clearly and without ambiguity:

> And [it so happened that] she in whose house he was living [conceived a passion for him and] sought to make him yield himself unto her; and she bolted the doors and said, "Come thou unto me!" [But Joseph] answered: "May God preserve me! Behold, goodly has my master made my stay [in this house]! Verily, to no good end come they that do [such] wrong!" (Yūsuf 12: 23)

> And, indeed, she desired him, and he desired her; [and he would have succumbed] had he not seen [in this temptation]

---

24. Ibid., p. 111.

an evidence of his Sustainer's truth: thus [We willed it to be]
in order that We might avert from him all evil and all deeds of
abomination – for, behold, he was truly one of Our servants.
And they both rushed to the door; and she [grasped and]
rent his tunic from behind-and [lo!] they met her lord at
the door! Said she: "What ought to be the punishment of one
who had evil designs on [the virtue of] thy wife – [what] but
imprisonment or a [yet more] grievous chastisement?"

[Joseph] exclaimed: "It was she who sought to make me yield
myself unto her!" Now one of those present, a member of
her own household, suggested this: "If his tunic has been torn
from the front, then she is telling the truth, and he is a liar;
but if his tunic has been torn from behind, then she is lying,
and he is speaking the truth."

And when [her husband] saw that his tunic was torn from
behind, he said: "Behold, this is [an instance] of your guile, O
womankind! Verily, awesome is your guile! [But,] Joseph, let
this pass! And thou, [O wife,] ask forgiveness for thy sin-for,
verily, thou hast been greatly at fault!" (*Yūsuf* 12: 23–29)

In the first part of this Qur'anic passage, one notes that it is clearly
a case of Zulaykha doing all she can to attempt to seduce Yusuf. The
latter seemed in fact to be embarrassed by this attempt but ended
up resisting the advances of this beautiful woman. He resisted as
best he could as is described in the Qur'an, since had it not been
for his invocation of one of the signs of the Creator, he might have
succumbed to her charms.

It is a sign from God which provoked the awakening of her
conscience at the very instant when he was about to flinch and
weaken, so bewitched was he by the charms of the lady of the
house. Some Qur'anic commentators have struggled to interpret
this temporary weakness displayed by Yusuf, indicated in the verse
through the phrase *'wa hamma biha'*; it was even unthinkable for
them that the idea could even have crossed his mind! This is due
to the fact that for a number of Muslim exegetes the Prophets were

infallible people, what we call *'ismat an-nubuwa'* or 'infallibility due to prophecy'.

And yet, one is surprised to see this *'isma* often interpreted as an annihilation of the humanity of the Prophets![25] The *'isma* or 'infallibility' of the Prophets was less in terms of renouncing their humanity but rather in their capacity for resistance and patience in times of struggle ... and it is precisely here that resides the merit of their human commitment in front of God.

Yusuf was not an angel. He was a human being who must have suffered, fought his carnal desires, undertaken a tremendous internal effort to control his negative impulses and vanquish this human attraction.

He was almost seduced because he was first and foremost a human being and his internal struggle was what allowed him to see the negative consequences which could result from his action. This was the Divine sign which suddenly enlightened Yusuf's torn heart ... God rewarded his efforts by reinforcing his faith, by protecting him and by stopping him from committing this doubly immoral act. Immoral on one side because he would have approached a woman who was forbidden to him and would have, on the other hand, betrayed the trust of the master in whose house he lived and whose unlimited favours he enjoyed.

Zulaykha thus seduced Yusuf and, as is described in the Qur'an, sought to unfairly accuse him at the very moment when she was caught in the act by her husband. She was soon nevertheless unmasked. Her husband seems to forgive[26] her since he asks Yusuf to forget the incident and sharply rebukes her through the words which have with time become the adage of those who want to denigrate all women: *'Inna kaydakunna 'azim'*, in other words: 'your female cunning are truly formidable.'

Al-kayd is a term which signifies in Arabic 'stratagem', 'machination', 'ruse' or also 'the effort in the undertaking of a task or a deed.' It is used several times in the Qur'an for diverse situations, imbued according to the situation with a positive

25. See *Al-Mar'a Bayna al-Qur'an* al-Ghannouchi, p. 42.
26. Tabari and *Tafsir* Ibn Kathir on Surah *Yusuf*.

or negative meaning. God in certain verses, describes Himself as possessing the power of *kayd*.[27]

In the same surah '*Yūsuf*', one finds the expression firstly in the shape of advice from a father to his son, Yusuf:

> *[Jacob] replied: "O my dear son! Do not relate thy dream to thy brothers lest [out of envy] they devise an evil scheme against thee; [...]" (Yūsuf 12: 5)*

And later, in a subsequent verse, one reads:

> *In this way did We contrive for Joseph [the attainment of his heart's desire [...] (Yūsuf 12: 76)*

Nonetheless, the term *kayd* takes on a truly horrifying meaning when it is placed in the context of Yusuf's seduction scene by al-'Aziz's wife! The *kayd* of Zulaykha then became the symbol of an audacious, illicit and perverse female temptation. With time, it took on an amplified significance in the Islamic psyche and was, thus, systematically associated with the image of women in general and her presumed predisposition to *kayd*, in other words to 'trickery' and 'fakery'!

And yet, the phrase '*inna kaydakunna 'azim*', as it was pronounced by Zulaykha's spouse – legitimately in this particular case – evokes first and foremost the bitterness and disappointment of a man betrayed by his spouse and who, to briefly alleviate his sorrow, articulated his resentment through this expression of a solemn sentence! The husband, offended by the indecent act of his wife, verbally responded in a manner which incriminated all women through Zulaykha. Annoyed in the moment, he essentializes his sentiment but he remains nonetheless very dignified and understanding since, despite being betrayed and disappointed by his wife's actions, he forgives her and asks her to repent.

The wording of this verse, which subtly describes the state of mind of al-'Aziz at the very moment the incident occurs, gives way, once removed from its context, to an incredible extrapolation and

---

27. See *al-A'raf* 7: 183 and *al-Ṭāriq* 86: 16.

becomes in time, a sacred word since it is imputed to God Himself as blaming women, all the women in the universe!

The reductive interpretation consistently given to this verse 'inna kaydakunna 'azim' has become with time and impassively the emblem of a Divine recommendation made to men in order to warn them of female duplicity. God is alleged to have affirmed in His Qur'an that women must be feared, all women, due to their dangerous capacity to trick and plot. It is this popular adage which has wreaked havoc for so long, and which lends credence to outlooks predisposed to this type of misogynistic interpretation. After the first charge of original sin unjustly attributed to the first woman of humanity, is added the responsibility carried by all women of the offence of Zulaykha, wife of al-'Aziz's subterfuge! An entire generation of Muslim scholars have long debated this concept of *kayd* and some have even gone so far as to claim that *kayd an-nisa* or the 'ruse of women' is far more dangerous than that of Satan, using arguments drawn from the Qur'an: Does God not say in His book: 'certainly, the ruse of Satan (*kayda ash-shaytan*) is weak.' Thus, the ruse of Satan is deemed relatively less dangerous compared to the *kayd* of women, which is *'azim* in other words, greater, or even more serious.[28]

This is how, every time there is any analysis of an event or an action, even the most anodyne action undertaken in relation to women, this verse is invoked as sacred proof of the confirmation of this Divine warning.[29] It becomes a veritable custom which makes this verse an inescapable maxim at the point of criticising women and which is found in virtually all Muslim societies.

And yet, nowhere in this story or anywhere else in the Qur'an, does God assert such a fact. It is all the more surprising to see in this specific story of Zulaykha the gulf which exists between the Qur'anic statement and given interpretations.

---

28. See *Al-Mar'a Bayna al-Qur'an* by al-Ghannoushi and his pertinent analysis on this misogynistic interpretation, p. 39.

29. In the Moroccan film *Keïd Ensa*, by Farida Belyazid, the director depicts this social reality using humour.

At no point in the Qur'anic narrative has God expressed a negative judgement, strictly speaking, of this woman even if she was, at a specific moment, certainly at fault and that her actions, which could be qualified as deception, led to as we see subsequently, Yusuf being unfairly imprisoned, which in and of itself is reprehensible.

The Qur'an does not judge this woman, it is content with commenting the incident, making an observation of the state of affairs at the time, while describing the scene in an extremely detailed manner and without for all that condemning the woman! Nowhere in the reading of these verses do we note a negative reference or even the most anodyne reproach towards Zulaykha.

The Qur'an seems to not wish to take a position. It is as if, while describing an act which is clearly reprehensible, the Qur'an is not judging its author and observes a silence which, in fact, speaks volumes about the Divine pedagogy and the approach of the Qur'an as concerns this sort of human conduct.

This is why one finds among other classical commentators a certain indulgence towards this woman and that Tabari reports, in order to clarify, the fact that Zulaykha's spouse did not engage with women: 'rajulun la ya'ti n-nisa'.[30]

It is worth noting also that in Western literature, Potiphar is said to have been a eunuch. Tabari refers to this disability in al-'Aziz in parallel to the beauty, youth and wealth of this woman! The great historian certainly does not draw any hasty conclusions, but appears to want to relativize Zulaykha's attitude while finding *en route* a number of excuses in order to support the Qur'an's lenient attitude towards her.

The Qur'anic story continues in this vein, always with this same sense of subtle kindness for Zulaykha and this is how we learn how this incident, which arose in the home of al-'Aziz, ends up being slyly divulged in all spheres of the society of the time and led to endless female gossip!

> NOW *the women of the city spoke [thus to one another]:*
> *"The wife of this nobleman is trying to induce her slave-boy*

---

30. Tabari, vol 1, p. 113.

to yield himself unto her! Her love for him has pierced her heart; verily, we see that she is undoubtedly suffering from an aberration!"

Thereupon, when she heard of their malicious talk, she sent for them, and prepared for them a sumptuous repast, and handed each of them a knife and said [to Joseph]: "Come out and show thyself to them!" And when the women saw him, they were greatly amazed at his beauty, and [so flustered were they that] they cut their hands [with their knives], exclaiming, "God save us! This is no mortal man! This is nought but a noble angel!"

Said she: "This, then, is he about whom you have been blaming me! And, indeed, I did try to make him yield himself unto me, but he remained chaste. Now, however, if he does not do what I bid him, he shall most certainly be imprisoned, and shall most certainly find himself among the despised!"
(*Yūsuf* 12: 30–32)

In this section of the story, the Qur'an emphasises the social context of the time, which could in fact easily be applied to other eras, by underlining the perverse effects of an over-represented elite, and underlining the perverse effects of a given elite represented, among other things, by idle women, bent on gossiping, living in the luxury and opulence of palaces. In this historical setting of an Egypt permeated by idolatry, steeped in immorality and hypocrisy, these women heartily criticized Zulaykha and relished her personal scandal, decrying in particular her crazy love for her poor servant, she the spouse of a rich and respected notable of the town.

It is interesting to note here firstly the description which is made in the Qur'an, through these women, of Zulaykha's love for Yusuf and which was apparently known to all. '*Shaghafaha hubban*' is an expression which is difficult to translate simply by 'in love'. It is in fact much stronger and more subtle than that!

In fact, Ibn 'Abbas speaks rather of 'the love which kills', *al-hub al-qatil* and explains that *shaghaf* symbolizes the most internal envelope of the heart. He also speaks of *hijab al-qalb*, or the veil of the heart.[31]

Zulaykha's love for Yusuf was so strong that it had penetrated the deepest part of her heart. A love which pierced the heart's internal veil! It is in this sense that a number of Muslim poets, particularly Persian poets, described the love of Zulaykha as a love which tears the veils of innocence.

Zulaykha was thus suffering from this love sickness which knows no age, nor time, nor era, a veritable sickness which has affected humanity from the dawn of time! The Persian poet Ar-Rumi immortalizes this love through the following verses:

> Love is like an ocean
> Upon which the skies are merely an ardent foam
> Like Zulaykha in her love for Yusuf

The great mystic Ibn 'Arabi, in his *Al-Futuhat al-Makkiyya*, depicts this legendary *love* as follows: 'It is said that Zulaykha was struck by an arrow and as her blood gradually flowed onto the earth, Yusuf's name became inscribed therein. She had repeated the name unconsciously so many times that it was flowing through her veins like blood ... .'

In Persian and Indo-Muslim mystical literature, Zulaykha has become a symbol of all those who are suffering. A passionate heroine, courageous and strong, for whom one feels a sense of compassion: 'The people always looked at the torn clothes of Yusuf ... but who saw the torn and battered heart of Zulaykha?'[32]

Thus Zulaykha felt truly hurt by the rumour-peddling of the women of the city who apparently could not understand what was happening to her, nor conceive what she was experiencing in the depths of her being!

What is more, the Qur'an openly criticizes the behaviour of these women since it speaks of '*makrihinna*'. *Al-makr* is a term which refers to treachery or deceit, and God therefore describes the

---

31. *Tafsir* Ibn Kathir, p. 450.
32. Ibid., p. 76.

behaviour of these women by this term *makr*, laden with meaning, to precisely highlight His reprobation towards this act which is defamatory, regardless of Zulaykha's actions being blameworthy in and of themselves. In other words, the Qur'an seems to affirm here that despite the indecency of Zulaykha's position, these women had no right to judge her, even less to slander her. And therein lies the message of the Divine pedagogy, which shows itself to be intransigent as concerns the private life of individuals and people's intimacy. Such is the behaviour which God enjoins, that of indulgence towards others, respect for intimacy, protection of morality. To be demanding of one's self but extremely indulgent with others is one of the fundamental qualities of the believer.

Unfortunately, the human tendency wants us to denounce or condemn others even when our own deficiencies are just as reprehensible or even worse and that our errors are often innumerable. How many women, particularly in our Muslim cultures very susceptible to this type of judgement, see themselves condemned for life, at times for fundamentally human errors, at others just on the basis of unfounded suspicions!

The Qur'anic text continues by describing Zulaykha as a woman doubly humiliated, in her self-esteem and in her honour, something which incites her to prepare a trick of her own which she plays on those who slandered her. She invites them to a banquet and for desert, serves them fruit, with knives to cut them. At that moment, she orders Yusuf to introduce himself to the guests and as soon as they set eyes on him, they are so blown away by his beauty that they inadvertently cut their hands, so thrown were they to see such splendour! They were so taken by the physique of this young man that they didn't even realize their wounds and, in an act of spontaneity, admit their error of judgement and recognize that this being must be the incarnation of an angel on earth since they had never seen comparable beauty!

In his interpretation Ibn Kathir[33] reports that Zulaykha commented on the attitude of these women in the following ironic terms: 'See what you have done to yourselves after only seeing

---

33. *Tafsīr* Ibn Kathir, p. 450.

Yusuf for a brief moment, how could you therefore blame me when I frequent him daily?' It is as if Zulaykha wanted to prove to the women and to the whole world if necessary, that her profound love for this man was grounded. In her madness, in a state of recklessness, and a moment of distraction, in her ardour ... at that moment all was justified in her eyes and like in these moments of human weakness nothing else is of importance. Zulaykha decided to follow through with her passion, and her despair ... This is how she ends in plain sight of these same women, threatening Yusuf to accept her advances and her love for him, or she'll send him to prison. A veritable psychological bribery to which Yusuf, ever protected by the Divine shield, the source of his great wisdom, refused to submit.

He prefers to sojourn in prison, despite his innocence, than to live imprisoned in the torment of forbidden passions and ephemeral love with an uncertain future ... These passionate moments which last but an instant, a cursed moment, which one regrets one's entire life and which ultimately leave only a sense of guilt or moral distress and bitterness. With great restraint he took his decision, proof of his dignity and faith, which the Qur'an outlines in the following terms:

> Said he: "O my Sustainer! Prison is more desirable to me than [compliance with] what these women invite me to: for, unless Thou turn away their guile from me, I might yet yield to their allure and become one of those who are unaware [of right and wrong]." (Yūsuf 12: 33)

Yusuf invoked God Most-Powerful in his aid. He knew himself to be weak and without defences and implored the Creator to support him and give him the strength to resist his leaning, as he admitted!

This illustrates more than anything else the real dimension of faith when it translates as strength and when it morphs into will. A faith which can certainly weaken, fail at certain occasions in life but which, if we know how to reinforce it, immunizes us against many temptations and which can protect us from our truly human shortcomings!

This is how Yusuf, despite his innocence, was imprisoned ... It was the price to pay and he was prepared to pay it because he knew himself to be supported by the Divine blessing. He underwent a multitude of struggles, recounted in detail in the surah, and finally, after a long journey, was promoted by the king of Egypt to the post of treasurer of the kingdom.

The Qur'an comments subsequently on how Yusuf was cleared, after an investigation undertaken under the aegis of the king on the reasons for his imprisonment and on the motivation for the wounds acquired by the women invited to Zulaykha's banquet.

And, thus Zulaykha admits her wrongs and publicly absolves Yusuf:

> [Thereupon the King sent for those women; and when they came,] he asked: "What was it that you hoped to achieve when you sought to make Joseph yield himself unto you?" The women answered: "God save us! We did not perceive the least evil [intention] on his part!" [And] the wife of Joseph's former master exclaimed: "Now has the truth come to light! It was I who sought to make him yield himself unto me – whereas he, behold, was indeed speaking the truth!"
>
> And yet, I am not trying to absolve myself: for, verily, man's inner self does incite [him] to evil, and saved are only they upon whom my Sustainer bestows His grace. Behold, my Sustainer is much forgiving, a dispenser of grace! (Yūsuf 12: 51–53)

One cannot read these verses without feeling profoundly touched by the emotion of this woman who admits her wrongs out loud and who proclaims the innocence of the one who had hurt her feelings and whom she had unjustly jailed ... One notes through this confession, publicly pronounced, the torment of guilt and the depth of repentance which emanates from inside this woman broken by passion.

Some classical commentators diverge on their interpretation of these last verses and attribute the latter words to Yusuf who evokes his 'master' and who spoke of the hazards of the human soul or *nafs*.[34]

Nonetheless the majority of scholars, including Ibn Kathir, affirm that it was Zulaykha who made a *mea culpa* in front of the Palace's aides, admitted her wrongs, rehabilitated Yusuf and the remainder of the words as they are reported in the Qur'an are without contest hers.

The section of the verse where she describes the disarray of her *nafs*, in other words of her 'soul' or 'inner self', and where she recognizes that the core of human nature is to lean towards bad (*inna n-nafsa la' ammaratun bi's-su'*) is recorded in Islamic hermeneutics as one of the three states of the human soul as described in the Holy Qur'an. In fact, the Qur'an speaks of the state of the soul known as *ammara bi's-su'*, that which orders evil or is subject to evil as verbalized by Zulaykha, that where the soul is *lawwama* or conscious of its weaknesses and always in search of perfection and finally where the soul is *mutma'inna*, in other words that which is living in serenity and the contentment of faith.

Zulaykha, as she is depicted by the Qur'an, personifies this *nafs* or 'human soul' which incites evil but which shows itself to be living through an internal struggle in order to purify itself, as is shown by the end of the Qur'anic story. This final scene as it is described in the Qur'an also testifies to the spiritual upheaval experienced by Zulaykha. After a lot of work on herself, she finishes by publicly repenting, convinced of the authenticity of the spiritual message transmitted by Yusuf.

Whereas the Qur'an, as the narrative progresses, describes a repentant Zulaykha, ravaged by guilt and suffering, and remains silent on the fate of this woman, the classical exegesis offers a less than romantic ending to the story.[35] In fact, once Yusuf was promoted to the higher tiers of the state, al-'Aziz is said to have died in murky circumstances and the Egyptian king of the time married

---

34. See the debate in *Tafsīr* Ibn Kathir, p.455.
35. Ibid.

Yusuf and Zulaykha with great pomp! Here is another romantic story which recalls that of another Qur'anic couple, namely *Solomon* and *Balkis*!

Finally, the profound and mystical dimension of this story resides in the illustration by the Qur'an of this immortal game of beauty and love! And as Sayyid Qutb says so well in his commentary, the Qur'an confronts us with a certain reality of human life, it describes human weaknesses, particularly those concerning physical urges, in order that we might be conscious that this message is aimed at humans with all their deficiencies and not to a community of angels![36]

The Qur'an also offers us here a lesson in humanity and clemency through the story of Zulaykha, this heroine despite herself, of forbidden love. Whereas a literalist reading condemns her unequivocally, declaring her to be the *eternal temptress*, even imputing to her the unchanging feminine responsibility for incitement to evil, the Qur'an, however, delicately describes her passion, her intense love, her suffering, and then her tough penitence and finally, her repentance brimming with truth and spirituality.

It is as if this sacred text sought to *deconstruct* this perpetual *fear of women*, this devastating concupiscence, by transmitting to us precisely the image of a woman who, via her purification through suffering, eternally personifies the true precariousness of our poor human soul, of our *nafs* ... And each time we re-read this verse on *nafs al-ammara bi s-su'i*, 'this soul which incites to evil', one should be reminded of the suffering of Zulaykha and through her of our inescapable human weakness ... .

Umm Musa and Asiah, the free women

The Qur'an does not speak of Musa's father. However, the mother of this Prophet beloved by God is cited in the sacred text under the name Umm Musa and plays a crucial role in the protection and education of this famous messenger of God.

The tradition[37] reports that Musa was born during those obscure

---

36. Annemarie Schimmel, see reference op. cit.
37. Tabari, *Tarikh*, 1: 6, p. 130.

moments in the history of humanity. In Egypt, the people of Israel were subjugated to a cruel slavery under the tyranny of Pharaoh. The latter is said to have had a dream which terrified him and had asked its interpretation to the soothsayers and wise men of the time who informed him that the vision was an omen concerning the imminent arrival of a Hebrew child who would overthrow his power, expulse him from his land and impose a new religion.

Enraged and fearful the dream might come to pass, Pharaoh ordered that all new-born Hebrew boys be put to death. It was in these dramatic conditions that Musa was born, at the heart of a cruel, ancient culture where the Pharaoh maintained the people of Israel in inhuman conditions, submitting them to a humiliating slavery.

The Qur'an repeatedly describes this episode in the story, while denouncing the despotism of Pharaoh and firmly condemning the absolute power which he symbolizes:

> We [now] convey unto thee some of the story of Moses and Pharaoh, setting forth the truth for [the benefit of] people who will believe. Behold, Pharaoh exalted himself in the land and divided its people into castes. One group of them he deemed utterly low; he would slaughter their sons and spare (only) their women: for, behold, he was one of those who spread corruption [on earth]. (al-Qaṣaṣ 28: 3–4)

Umm Musa bore her child when Pharaoh had already ordered the murder of thousands of Hebrew boys. She sought in vain to hide his birth, tormented by the fear of seeing her son experience the same fate. But how to hide the birth of this little boy when Pharaoh's regime and its acolytes were mobilized *en masse* to identify the arrival of any male birth at the heart of the people of Israel?! A terrible ordeal for the heart of this poor mother! When she found herself in a state of anguish and fear at the thought of losing her child, and not knowing what to do in order to save him from Pharaoh's hands, Umm Musa received Divine revelation! God told her, from atop the seven skies, to place her son in a 'casket', *tabut*, and to place it on the banks of the Nile.

> *When We inspired thy mother with this inspiration: Place him*
> *in a chest and throw it into the river, and thereupon the river*
> *will cast him ashore, [and] one who is an enemy unto Me*
> *and an enemy unto him will adopt him. "And [thus early]*
> *I spread Mine Own love over thee – and [this] in order that*
> *thou might be formed under Mine eye." (al-Qaṣaṣ* 28: 7)

This is indeed a message of consolation and appeasement that the Creator sent to this woman in order that she might arm herself with patience and demonstrate endurance and firmness when faced with this agony with which she was confronted ... God Himself, in His immeasurable softness, asked her not to fear, not to be sad, to believe in Him and in His generosity.

Through these verses, He was transmitting two messages to her: on one hand, He was relieving her heart by promising her the certain return of her child: '*We will return him to you.*' On the other hand, He was predicting to her the future of her son who appeared to be destined by the Creator to become one of His greatest Prophets. The Divine revelation gave her two reasons not to be sad. Despite her love for her child, she was able to control her fear and appease her maternal heart, thanks to this wonderful and happy Divine consolation. God, while understanding her profound distress, encouraged her to endure, to hope, to be patient again and again ... The Qur'anic description of Umm Musa's emotional experience is of sublime beauty and the words of the Creator towards this woman are of an infinite tenderness:

> *On the morrow, however, an aching void grew up in the*
> *heart of the mother of Moses, and she would indeed have*
> *disclosed all about him had We not endowed her heart with*
> *enough strength to keep alive her faith [in Our promise].*
> *(al-Qaṣaṣ* 28: 10)

In this passage, the Qur'an describes in a very studied fashion the heart of this woman, which had become 'empty' after the separation from her son. The Arabic term *farighan* can be translated as 'emptied' or, 'dried up'. The description is very subtle and the metaphor used by the Qur'an here seeks to demonstrate the extent to which the sadness of this woman was profound. Her heart was emptied of all except for Musa ... Nothing else mattered in her eyes, life no longer had meaning and only the memory of her child remained bright in her heart ... The suffering was such that at every instant she was on the verge of crying out from her pain, divulging the secret and telling all. She was on the verge of betraying herself had it not been for the resoluteness which God inspired in her heart in order that she might persist in her conviction. This force which God instilled in her and which the Qur'an translates subtly with the word *rabatna*, a term which signifies in Arabic 'attach' or 'bandage'. The struggle was so great that it was necessary for God to 'attach' his feelings in order to stop their *bursting* in daylight.

God, in His profound clemency, supported this woman, accompanied her in her distress and pushed her to remain firm, to be strong and to conquer her maternal fears. He consolidated his faith and belief and protected her in these difficult moments through His infinite compassion ... and thanks to God, she was able to remain serene and patient.

Meanwhile, the ark transporting the little Musa reached the banks of the gardens of Pharaoh's palace. He was taken in by his wife, Asiah who, moved by this baby sent like a blessing from above – the tradition states she was herself barren – begged Pharaoh not to kill him and to allow her to keep him as her child.

> And [some of] Pharaoh's household found [and spared] him: for [We had willed] that he becomes an enemy unto them and [a source of] grief, seeing that Pharaoh and Haman and their hosts were sinners indeed! Now the wife of Pharaoh said: "A joy to the eye [could this child be] for me and thee! Slay him not: he may well be of use to us, or we may adopt him as a son!" And they had no presentiment [of what he was to become]. (al-Qaṣaṣ 28: 8–9)

Meanwhile, Umm Musa asked her daughter Maryam to follow the traces of her young brother and to keep an eye on all that happened around him. This is how Maryam learnt that the newborn was refusing all his wet nurses and was on the verge of dying. The entire entourage of the palace was in turmoil in search of a wet nurse to save Asiah, wife of Pharaoh's little protégé, who was distressed at the thought of losing the one who had come to fill the maternal void in her life. The Divine plan was underway slowly and impassively ... . does God not say in His Holy Qur'an:

> Now from the very beginning We caused him to refuse the breast of [Egyptian] nurses [...] (al-Qaṣaṣ 28: 12)

Maryam, moved by this opportunity and taking advantage of the confusion prevailing around this event, suggested timidly but nonetheless very cleverly, a wet nurse which the child would not reject! And this was how the baby was returned to Umm Musa who, in the face of general stupor, nursed the child with ease, while trying to simultaneously disguise her immense joy at being reunited with her small beloved ... God is Great and Merciful and one part of His promise was being realized!

Invited to live at the palace by Asiah in order to become the official wet nurse of the newborn, Umm Musa respectfully refused the request and offered to keep the child with her while he required nursing, justifying her refusal through the fact she had other children whom she could not leave alone. Umm Musa was conscious of the power she had at that moment, that of being the only woman who was able to nurse Asiah's young protégé! Through this she had the supreme opportunity to impose her will and, in retrieving the child in order to feed him, she was simply taking back her due! At home and away from the view of others, she was free to demonstrate her maternal love as she saw fit, without the palace entourage watching her. Asiah could only accept in the face of Umm Musa's tenacity, aware of her power in the situation. Umm Musa was motivated by the strength she drew from her conviction and her trust in the pact she had made with God: 'We will return him to you.' He had promised to return his son and he was there, safe and sound in her arms ... God always keeps His promises!

And it was His providence which was being played out. Umm Musa, honoured by these Divine gifts, was simply content ... She was doubly so, firstly through her reunion with her child and also by the intense happiness of feeling chosen, her, this humble and modest woman, by the Creator of this world! The Qur'an describes this episode in these terms:

> *And thus We restored him to his mother, so that her eye might he gladdened, and that she might grieve no longer, and that she might know that God's promise always comes true – even though most of them know it not!* (al-Qaṣaṣ 28: 13)

Musa, as God had promised, returned to his original home, fed and surrounded by that maternal tenderness which transmitted the necessary affection for his psychological wellbeing and gave him at the same time the strength to resist trials ... all manner of trials. If we had to retain a moral from the story of Umm Musa, it would be beyond the strength of emotion of a mother, courage, as well as resistance to oppression ... a resistance which Umm Musa never ceased to express thanks to her spiritual powers which are her faith in God, trust in His destiny and endurance ... . She was able to brave, thanks to God, Pharaoh's hegemonic will.

These are the lessons to take from the story of Umm Musa as it is told by the Qur'an ... A woman who, strengthened from received revelation, held strong against the evil forces embodied by Pharaoh and his authoritarian power.

She knew herself to be invested by a grandiose mission, that of preparing her child to receive a message destined for humanity in its entirety, a message of liberation. Musa had to liberate his people from slavery and the servitude in which they would be constrained by this deified man who was Pharaoh and who embodied tyranny in all its cruelty.

Tyranny of the sort which can be found all along the history of humanity, in all times and all civilizations and against which God never ceased to warn human beings ... This is how Musa was raised by his real mother, educated to never abdicate in the face of injustice and to refuse all forms of human oppression.

Musa also had the particular destiny of having been raised concomitantly by another woman of great notoriety, Asiah, who became in some ways his adoptive mother.

Asiah, wife of Pharaoh, as we have already seen, was strongly taken by the child that had come to fill the lack of affection of which she had cruelly suffered, bullied as she was by her authoritarian husband. The Qur'an describes her as an exemplary woman:

> And for those who have attained to faith God has propounded a parable in [the story of] Pharaoh's wife as she prayed 'O my Sustainer! Build Thou for me a mansion in the paradise [that is] with Thee, and save me from Pharaoh and his doings, and save me, from all evildoing folk! (al-Taḥrīm 66: 11)

She was thus among the women whom the Qur'an erects as a spiritual ideal for all believers, a feminine example of this sublimated belief ... a belief born at the heart of all disbelief.

Asiah, like Umm Musa, made resistance to Pharaoh's dictatorial powers her warhorse, throughout her entire life. Living in opulence, luxury and the splendour of the palace of one of the greatest tyrants known to humanity, she, nonetheless, knew how to preserve herself from all the dangers associated with this sort of life and dedicate herself to the worship of the One God.

Constrained to live under the yoke of this authority, she armed herself with endurance, faith and renunciation. This allowed her to attain the rank of human perfection as the Prophet Muhammad said of her in a famous hadith.

Whereas everyone was prostrating in front of Pharaoh and glorifying his reign and power, Asiah refused this slavery and proclaimed her refusal to adhere to his despotic logic. She opposed his diktat despite her powerlessness and impotence in the face of the despotic force of this leader.

She proclaimed loudly and proudly her faith in God and dared to break the laws of the time, which considered Pharaoh as God on earth. Asiah, through her spiritual revolt, lived in continuous confrontation against the power in place and despite her solitude, her destitution and suffering, she contested the established order throughout her entire life: that of injustice and oppression.

It was her also who must have engraved this love of justice and freedom in the spirit and education of Musa ... .

Born between these two model mothers, between these two worlds which everything seemed to separate, Musa forged himself a strong personality, full of wisdom and strength of character.

He was put, through God's will, under the protection of these two exceptional women, to prepare him, messenger of God, to contest the symbols of tyranny, of oppression and of slavery. Two women seemingly free since they opposed servility, injustice and human exploitation ... each living in distinct environments but nourished by the same spiritual certainty, they taught him to resist the terror of absolutist power and to transmit to his people the message of dignity and freedom as required by their Creator ... .

They loved their son unreservedly, protected him tenderly, defended him until the end, all the while educating him and preparing him to be what he would become, a liberating Prophet for men ... and women.

The daughter of Shuʿayb and the meeting with Musa

During one of the many escapades experienced by Prophet Musa during his life, the Qur'an relates his meeting, in the Madyan desert, with two young women near a water fountain. In fact, Musa left Pharaoh's court in Egypt during his adulthood, in order to go and live among his people, the Hebrews. Having seen an Egyptian man mistreating one of his people, he killed him with his bare hands. Fearing punishment for the murder, he sought refuge in the desert of Madyan in Jordan where nomadic tribes lived. It is there where the infamous meeting occurred:

> NOW WHEN he arrived at the wells of Madyan, he found
> there a large group of men who were watering [their herds
> and flocks]; and at some distance from them he came upon

*two women who were keeping back their flock. He asked
[them]: "What is the matter with you?" They answered: "We
cannot water [our animals] until the herdsmen drive [theirs]
home – for [we are weak and] our father is a very old man."*

*So he watered [their flock] for them: and when he withdrew
into the shade and prayed: "O my Sustainer! Verily, in dire
need am I of any good which Thou mayest bestow upon me!"*

*[Shortly] afterwards, one of the two [maidens] approached
him, walking shyly, and said: "Behold, my father invites thee,
so that he might duly reward thee for thy having watered [our
flock] for us." And as soon as [Moses] came unto him and
told him the story [of his life], he said: "Have no fear! Thou
art now safe from those evildoing folk!"*

*Said one of the two [daughters]: "O my father! Hire him: for,
behold, the best [man] that thou couldst hire is one who is
[as] strong and worthy of trust [as he]!"*

*[After some time, the father] said: "Behold, I am willing to let
thee wed one of these two daughters of mine on the understanding
that thou wilt remain eight years in my service [...]"*
(al-Qasas 28: 23–27)

The old man in question here, as well as his two daughters, appear
to be mysterious characters. In fact, no authentic references
confirm that the elderly man cited was Prophet Shu'ayb as is often
understood in the classical literature. But as Tabari clarifies, the
vast majority of *ulema* believe it was in fact Shu'ayb, cited elsewhere
in other Qur'anic passages as the Prophet of the Madyan people.
Some scholars claim he was in fact the nephew of Shu'ayb, whereas
for others, who draw in the ancient monotheistic traditions, the
elderly man was a saintly man of the time named Jethro.[38]

What is more, we find this episode in Musa's life in the Bible, in
the book of Exodus, where the elderly man in question, father to

---

38. On this issue, see the discussion by Sayyid Qutb, *Fi Zilal al-Qur'an*, vol. 5,
p. 2,787.

two young women, is a priest known as Jethro.[39]

The Bible evokes Musa's intervention in Madyan country when two shepherds sought to impede the access of Jethro's daughters to a well. Musa came to their rescue and watered their livestock. Still according to the Bible, Musa married Sephora, one of Jethro's daughters. We find in the classical exegesis the same narrative with a few variations.[40]

From the first Qur'anic verses, we note the extreme thoughtfulness and courtesy of Musa who, arriving on the scene, was moved and touched to see two young women with their herd prevented from approaching the well, when all the other people were watering their livestock, without worrying themselves in the slightest with the fate of these two individuals.

Despite being himself a stranger in these lands, while these young women were seemingly from these people, he felt that they were ultimately a bit like him, just as much strangers as he was and this sense of solidarity, among other things, seems to have motivated him implicitly to help them and to offer them his assistance.[41] Musa was exhausted after his long trip from Egypt and the torments of life which rendered him a roaming refugee in the desert of Madyan. It is from this place which his sad invocation of God comes, where he shares with Him his weakness, his exhaustion and his impotence: 'God, I am lacking in all of which you have favoured me.' And then, as if by magic, God sends him a message of hope, as only God knows how … In the depths of our despair, He alone knows how to send us Signs which illuminate our hearts … .

This is how Musa, sinking into bitterness and despondency, felt his life become illuminated by a mere presence … One of the young women, full of gentleness and delicacy, approached him reservedly and shyly asking him to follow her to her father's, the latter wishing to thank him for his assistance.

Musa saw himself invited, he who just minutes prior was feeling alone in the world and had confided in his Lord about his solitude

---

39. Bible, Exodus, chapter 2: 16.
40. *Tafsīr* Ibn Kathir
41. *Tafsīr* of al-Qushayri.

and total destitution. The elderly man listened to Musa's story attentively and sympathising, offered him his hospitality while assuring him of his protection and that of his people.

As the Qur'an narrates, one of the young women urged her father to hire the services of this young man by describing him as 'strong and worthy of trust.' The classical Qur'anic exegesis interprets the characteristics of 'strong and worthy of trust' through a series of commentaries relating to Musa's physical strength and his chaste attitude towards the young women. The hermeneutical tradition states that in order to help them water their flock, Musa had to lift a rock which covered the well and which could only be lifted by twenty, even forty men. As for his rectitude, it is explained by his prudence and great restraint vis-à-vis the young woman accompanying him on the journey to the elderly man's abode. This is how, and according to the classical commentaries, that Musa asked the young woman to walk behind him and guide him by throwing stones on the path he should follow. Others report that while accompanying him, the wind lifted a section of the young woman's dress, which led Musa to ask her to walk behind him on the path. These are the explanations which we find in the great majority of classical commentaries concerning the virtues and merits of Musa.[42]

Musa was 'strong' because he apparently had prodigious physical capabilities and his rectitude and seriousness were illustrated in his way of accompanying the young woman! This is why, according to the classical exegesis, that the elderly man offered him work and even to marry him to one of his daughters.

In his *tafsīr* 'Fi Zilal al-Qur'an', Sayyid Qutb criticizes this sort of commentary which he argues refers to useless details with no place here and which he considers to be tainted by affectation and pretension.[43] He considers that the commentators could have avoided such descriptions which ultimately add very little to a story which is itself sufficiently clear and transparent.

---

42. *Tafsīr* of the verse in question: Tabari, Ibn Kathir, al-Jalalayn, al-Qurṭubi, al-Baydawi.
43. *Tafsīr* of Sayyid Qutb, vol 5, p. 2,788.

Neither Musa nor this young woman, whom the Qur'an describes as advancing with timidity *bi-istihya'*, need all these *forced* explanations to prove their irreproachable moral behaviour.

The Qur'anic verses, while being simple and concise, tell us far more in the profound significance of the teachings we should retain than these supposed clarifications which, in this case for example, are rather simplistic, even infantilising. Whereas the Qur'anic meaning goes beyond these vain and puerile details, certain classical commentaries remain prisoners of a reductive vision which lingers on futilities, when the finalities of the verse go beyond this type of ultimately very base sentiments.

The Qur'an has in fact not given any details as regards the meeting of these two individuals. But thanks to its very particular style, it uses subtle allusions, called *ishārāt*, which alone are sufficient to direct us towards the intention of the text. In these precise verses, the different allusions made contain sufficient clues to perceive that the scene was not fortuitous and that the *something* which happened between Musa and one of the young women was both noble and spontaneous all at once.

The Qur'an describes the magic of this moment with simple and studied terminology: the encounter around a fountain ... . Musa's bravery ... the portrait painted by the young woman to her father ... the modest yet determined young woman ... her very courteous invitation ... Words which illustrate without saying them the meeting of two hearts suddenly linked through an implicit understanding based on trust, spontaneity and feelings, still confused, but very innocent ... .

One can not read these words without perceiving the romantic story unfolding behind these sober, subtle, yet intense words: the sadness of this errant man whom Musa had been for several days, his great emotion at the sight of these girls excluded through a difficult social environment and the dazzling effect of she who, impressed by the beauty of the young stranger's soul, urged her father to keep him by them, in their home, near her especially ... .

The young woman appreciated the nobility of this unknown man who was more proactive and obliging than the individuals

from her own people. Despite her *timidity* or, *modesty* as described
in the Qur'an, she suggested to her father to hire his services ... *'he
is strong and worthy of trust'* she tells him. The message is clear in the
eyes of this elderly man. She need not say any more, it could be
read in her eyes such was the emotion which she struggled to hide.
The old man was quickly convinced of the probity and loyalty of
this valiant foreigner as he listened to his story, and offered him
his daughter in marriage with the greatest simplicity and a natural
frankness ... . he was merely transmitting the message of the woman
herself!

The father, the elderly sage he was, had understood that between
these two young people, something had happened ... a sort of
emotional and spiritual communion ... a spontaneous emotional
inclination and a reciprocal complicity which we might refer to
today in modern parlance as *love at first sight*!

And the Qur'an describes all this plainly and without any
pretence because there is no shame in expressing one's feelings,
in revealing the noblest of intentions and in manifesting one's
emotions when they are sincere and true. This is perhaps the crux
of what must be retained from the story of Musa and his future
spouse. The spontaneity of a meeting, the discovery of a kindred
spirit, gestures which speak louder than the most beautiful love
serenades ... The greatness of emotions which express themselves in
acts of kindness and generosity ... .

The young woman whom Musa married is described in one
exegesis commentary as being endowed with a 'chivalrous spirit',
furussiya. In fact, according to Ibn Mas'ud and reported by Sufyan
ath-Thawri, three people are endowed with *furussiya*: Abu Bakr as-
Siddiq, known for his noble and loyal behaviour, al-'Aziz, the man
who adopted Prophet Yusuf and who demonstrated clemency and
generosity towards this Prophet, and the daughter of Shu'ayb for
having described Musa as being 'strong and worthy of trust'. The
sentence has since become the equivalent of a much used adage in
religious terms, but sadly one regrets the omission of the entire
affective and emotional aspect of the saying which has been
neglected, even depreciated. The heartfelt emotions of a young

woman who was merely expressing her most noble sentiments is often overlooked through this verse, in other words, one who made her declaration of love to this chosen Prophet with the greatest of sincerity ... .

Maryam, the favourite

Of all the female characters mentioned in the Qur'an, Maryam is without doubt she who remains the most famous and whose undeniable universal renown transcends all traditions and cultures. Tolerated by some, venerated to the point of idolatry by others, respected and honoured by many, she appears to be among the rare case of figures around whom there has been, throughout the history of humanity, a degree of consensual agreement.

Maryam, a link between Christians and Muslims

Through my understanding of the Qur'an, in general, and as pertains to verses relative to Christians, to Christ, to Mary and to monks in particular, I began to realise that I possess a share in the book of God: It is not strange to me, nor am I a stranger to it [...] it is my book as it is the book of Muslims [...] Through my share, I consider it addressed from its origin to all human beings who believe in God and in the last day ... .

These beautiful words are those of a believing Christian[44], stunned to see, among other things, how Maryam, or, Mary, as she is known in the Christian tradition, is glorified and honoured by the sacred text of Muslims.

If we had to seek a single point of convergence between the two traditions, Christian and Muslim, we would without doubt have opted unanimously for Maryam, mother of 'Isa (Jesus). On this historical personality, there doesn't appear to be any fundamental disagreements and whoever reads the scriptural sources of the two traditions would be stupefied to see so many similarities, particularly for those who believe erroneously that Islam can only

---

44. Nasri Salhab, *L'Islam, tel que je l'ai connu; au religion de la clemence et de la paix,* , (Rabat: l'Organisation islamique pour l'Education, les Sciences et la Culture, 2003)., chapter III.

be a source of animosity and rejection of the other ... all others!

In this regard, Maryam seems to be a veritable link between Muslims and Christians and symbolizes par excellence, this spiritual bridge which resuscitates a monotheism typically headed by the ancestor of the Prophets, Ibrahim. A woman highly privileged by the Creator who 'revives the monotheistic testimony of which Abraham constitutes the universally recognized figure, but she does so as a woman, which adds, according to the Qur'an, a new proximity with the mystery of God.'[45]

In this masculine Islamic horizon, she is inscribed as a woman who enjoys an eternal perfection, which confers upon her, according to the Qur'anic vision, a particularly high rank, namely that of Prophetic dignity.[46]

It is true, and we do not recognize this enough as Muslims, that the Qur'an elevates Maryam to a level unparalleled by any other woman in history. The Muslim mystical tradition qualifies Maryam's position as being predestined, a woman with an exceptional vocation and enjoying a pre-eternal election.[47]

She is also the only one to be mentioned in the Qur'an by her first name, undeniable evidence of her proximity to God! She also benefits from the predilection accorded to her family, namely to the family of 'Imran:[48]

> BEHOLD, God raised Adam, and Noah, and the House of
> Abraham, and the House of Imran above all mankind, in
> one line of descent. And God was all-hearing, all-knowing.
> (Āl 'Imrān 3: 33–34)

The birth of Maryam

With the birth of Maryam, humanity enters a new epoch and one of its final revelations. It is the eve of a profound spiritual renewal which remains for ever engraved in the memory of history ... This

---

45. Michel Dousse, *Marie la musulmane*, (Paris: Albin Michel, 2005, p. 207.)
46. Concept used by Pierre Lory in his excellent study on *Mary, mother of Jesus in mystical Muslim exegeses*, May 2005, Freud-Lacan.com.
47. Ibid.
48. Ibid.

is how the Holy Qur'an celebrates the coming into this world of Maryam, one of the most important women, if not *the most important* woman that humanity has ever known and whose spiritual journey remains without doubt one of the most beautiful in the world ... .

The story of Maryam's nativity, as it is told in the Qur'an, begins with the invocation of the woman who bore her and who is mentioned under the name of *imra'atuu*: "*Imran*, 'the wife of 'Imran'. Maryam's mother, called Hanna by historians or Anne according to Christian tradition, is described as a firm believer who, following a long period of infertility and numerous pleas aimed at her Creator, saw her wish for a child granted at an advanced age in her life. Overwhelmed by happiness at the news of her much desired pregnancy, she made a wish of consecration of the child to come to God, as a measure of her recognition and infinite gratitude. This is how the Qur'an describes the episode:

> When a woman of [the House of] 'Imran prayed: 'O my Sustainer! "Behold, unto Thee do I vow [the child] that is in, my womb, to be devoted to Thy service. Accept it, then, from me: verily, Thou alone art all-hearing, all-knowing!"
> (Āl 'Imrān 3: 35)

Hanna, a profoundly religious woman, wished ardently to *offer* her future child to God which, translated in the language of the time, equated to saying that he would be entirely dedicated to the service of the sacred temple. In fact, according to the traditions of the time, the Jewish ritual offered the possibility of dedicating, from birth, young children to the service of the sanctuary, but these could only be boys due to – again according to the customs of the time – women's menstruations, which were considered a source of impurity. One notes that throughout time and the history of humanity, discrimination against the female gender is widely found and is felt all the more acutely in the sacred domain, erroneously perceived as the male prerogative by Divine writ! According to the logic of the mores of the time, in order to concretize her pledge, Hanna *had* to bear a boy in order for him to accomplish this religious mission specifically assigned to the most virtuous of men. She thus dreamt of seeing her future child among the faithful of God, those who were among the chosen of the city. She wanted her child to be *muharraran*, in other words free and freed from the slavery of this world. The Qur'anic exegesis in both its classical[49] and mystical variants, expresses Hanna's aspiration to see her future child freed from the dependence of negative passions and the demands of his carnal soul.

She wanted him totally dedicated to God's love, to His obedience and at the service of His friends, of His worshippers, those who lived in the sacred house.[50] This is the same interpretation favoured by Sayyid Qutb who describes the mother of Maryam as a pious soul who, in offering the fruit of her loin to her Creator, was offering us through her actions a beautiful lesson in *human liberation*. She wanted him freed from all except Him ... It is the perfect translation of submission to God, the sublime image of profound adherence to the principle of Divine unicity or, *tawḥīd* ... .

But how great was her surprise during the birth of her child when she realizes that God had given her girl! How could a girl negotiate this religious role, the exclusive privilege of the masculine gender?! Hanna appears, in a first instance, a little disappointed to have birthed a daughter. The Qur'an describes the hardly veiled sadness of this mother at seeing herself birth a 'poor daughter', when she had promised to dedicate her future child, a boy as was required, to this religious consecration of the time. Distraught, she apologizes to her Lord:

> But when she had given birth to the child, she said: 'O my Sustainer! Behold, I have given birth to a female' – all the while God had been fully aware of what she would give birth to, and [fully aware] that no male child [she might have hoped for] could ever have been like this female – 'and I have named her Mary. And, verily, I seek Thy protection for her and her offspring against Satan, the accursed. (Āl 'Imrān 3: 36)

---

49. *Tafsīr* by Ibn Kathir, Tabari, al-Qurṭubi, etc.
50. Sahl al-Tustari, *Tafsīr al-Qur'an al'-Azim*, cited in *Mary, mother of Jesus* Lory.

Hanna was thus saddened, disappointed, but she was especially scared of disappointing her Creator and of not being able to accomplish her promise. Nonetheless, one glimpses through her sad disappointment a sense of latent rebellion faced with the injustice of this discriminatory practise which she expressed to God in the shape of a personal complaint: '*A boy is not the same as a girl*' an observation which she evokes bitterly in front of God ... Hanna was complaining about this established social order which forbade women from accessing this religious authority! In this intimate discussion with God, Hanna laments, confides and implores her Creator ... She wants to believe to the end that her wish of consecration could come about, even with a daughter! She implores God to accept the child and to preserve her: '*I named her Maryam and place her oh Lord under Your protection.*' In the language of the time, Maryam signified the devoted or the servant of God. Hanna was expressing through this name her determination, but also her trust in the Divine response.

The classical exegesis[51] attributes the verse 'God knew well what she had born' to God Himself, who responds to Hanna's lament by assuring her that in fact this daughter that He has bestowed upon her was infinitely better than the boy she had hoped for and that what was in store for her was far removed from what she had aspired to for her much anticipated son!

Hanna's wish is granted and God affirms it in the following verse:

> And thereupon her Sustainer accepted the girl-child with goodly acceptance, and caused her to grow up in goodly growth [...] (*Āl 'Imrān* 3: 37)

Despite the fact that the status of *muharraran*, in other words that of 'consecration' to the sacred temple, was devolved to boys alone, God chose a girl and granted her this religious preference, so coveted, and habitually afforded only to the select *men* of the time. God thus explicitly elects a woman to remedy the discriminatory situation of

---

51. Zamakhshari *Al-Kashaf*.

the era and to demonstrate to human beings that ultimately, it isn't a question of *gender* but rather of *virtue* and *piety*. And Maryam was without doubt she who personified the universal reference to this human piety, drawing the amazement of her contemporaries and of all human beings whatever their époque ... .

Certain commentators and Muslim thinkers have nonetheless extracted the verse: '*A boy is not like a girl*' (*wa laysa al-dhakar ka'l-untha*) out of its historical context and have attributed to it an interpretation which goes against the actual meaning intended by the Qur'an.

In fact, given that it was about redressing an injustice, as previously stated, and, thus, of abolishing a sexist tradition of the era, some have instead used the verse as *a justification* to religiously buttress a proclaimed *preponderance* of men over women.[52]

Despite the Divine words being absolutely clear, in other words correcting, even contesting, an unjust tradition of the time, some interpreters have remained locked in an unfortunate cultural misogyny and have claimed that this verse is a Divine affirmation of the superiority of men over women.

Most alarming is that the argumentation used by the latter is almost laughable if not ridiculous since some try and *explain* the inferiority of women – affirmed, according to them, by this same verse – by the fact that the latter are not required to catch up the fasting days during the month of Ramadan, in cases of sexual relations during the daytime – normally forbidden during the fast – whereas men are required to![53] One fails to see the rationale or logic of such a statement, but the fact is it is reproduced in black and white in the great works of classical exegesis! Whereas others, still in order to legitimize the superiority of men, get mired in eternal justifications of menstruations and the physiological transformations which, according to their way of seeing things, render woman a *biologically inferior* being, even *incomparable* to man who was spared all these human *impurities*. Biological and natural

---

52. See the commentary made on this subject by al-Ghannoushi, *Al-Mar'a Bayna al-Qur'an*, p. 26.
53. *Tafsir* of al-Qurtubi.

differences are confused with pre-eminence and supremacy. This biological difference constitutes the bulk of the argumentation of those who advocate inequality between women and men.

Man and woman are of course *distinct* in their physical structures but this doesn't imply the superiority of one over the other. This vision is undoubtedly *differentiating*, but certainly not discriminatory. To be a woman or a man is to merely be other, without being inferior one compared to the other, and the recognition of the right to equality is inseparable from the right to difference. One sees, therefore, how the interpretation of a verse which is intended to *redress* an unjust tradition towards women becomes in fact an alibi for a cultural discrimination which seeks to be faithful to the principles of Islam!

Through this story of the birth of Maryam, God doubly celebrates women. Firstly by *fulfilling* a mother's wishes, a fervent believer, who doesn't hesitate to deplore, during an intimate imploration of her Lord, a sexist tradition of the time and then, by preordaining the daughter Maryam to this role of chosen-woman. The mother and the daughter, two women, who find themselves honoured and fulfilled by the Creator ... .

Hanna, in calling on the Creator to accept her daughter as among the *freed* human beings, transmitted this hymn of deliverance to the whole of humanity. Maryam will be born freed of all constraints. And, through her *liberation*, God transmits a message to women and men of this earth, in order that they might free themselves of all forms of servitude. This is without doubt where the profound meaning of the Islamic vision for human liberation lies ... .

Maryam's spiritual retreat
In conformity with the wishes of her mother and the promise of 'protection' affirmed by the Creator, Maryam grew up in a universe of piety, of spirituality and of devotion. She was known among her people for her abnegation and her devotion to God, and since she carried within her the signs of Divine predilection, all the high religious authorities of her time stridently concurred in view of

adopting this person chosen by God.[54]

The honour came to Zakariyyah, a known and venerated Prophet of the time, who took Maryam under his tutelage and took charge of her spiritual education. In fact, in accordance with a custom of the time, the person caring for the sacred temple had to be taken charge of by a priest in order that the latter might guide him and direct him in his monastic life. Maryam had the best of guides, more than a priest, hers was a Prophet of the stature of Zakariyyah, who undertook this mission, that of educating her spiritually and ensuring her protection, while guaranteeing the means of subsistence necessary in order to allow her to lead a peaceful life in the Sanctuary. Maryam outstripped all her predecessors through her profound piety and fervent meditation but also apparently, according to the stories of the time, through the mysterious arrival of *Divine gifts*, which each day were in all likelihood intended for her ... These particular daily *gifts* ended up surprising and even amazing Zakariyyah, despite him being a Prophet and normally accustomed to these sorts of spiritual experiences! This is what the following verse conveys:

> *Whenever Zachariah visited her in the sanctuary, he found her provided with food. He would ask: "O Mary, whence came this unto thee?' She would answer: 'It is from God; behold, God grants sustenance unto whom He wills, beyond all reckoning." (Āl 'Imrān 3: 37)*

The majority of classical exegeses almost invariably translate the word *rizq* as 'wealth or fortune, in food'. They also report based on ancient pre-Islamic sources the fact that every time Zakariyyah came to visit Maryam, he found her with, 'summer fruits in winter and winter fruits in summer'. The bulk of this 'richness' which Maryam was blessed with was summarized, according to certain commentators, by *out of season fruits* which were said to have engendered the fascination of Prophet Zakariyyah!

---

54. *Āl 'Imrān* 3: 44

The jurist Rashid Rida rightly contests, and in this case in particular, this type of textual reproduction of ancient tests which, while adding very little of use to the believer ensure the perpetuation of fanciful legends which, in the long run, risk voiding the content of the Qur'anic story from its real and profound significance.[55] Nonetheless, one finds in the collection by Ibn Kathir a single reading which stands out from the rest and which consists in interpreting this enigmatic *rizq* as rather being a *source of knowledge and understanding* or *'ilm*, transcribed on parchment and manuscripts: *suhuf fiha 'ilm*. This confirms one of the mystical exegeses which suggests that these 'supplies' referred in fact to *spiritual nourishment* (*rizq ruhani*), stemming from Divine hospitality towards Maryam.[56] She was receiving the Knowledge and understanding as a Divine gift in order to strengthen her heart and sharpen her intellect ... .

It is clear that the latter interpretations are more consistent with the general significance of the Qur'anic vision, which encourages knowledge as an inexhaustible foundation of spiritual and material renewal. A source able to lead and guide the believer towards a better understanding of the world and its Creator. And, in this case, Maryam was the perfect example of erudition who, isolated in her spiritual renewal, *nourished herself* on this infinite Divine Knowledge ... It is precisely this extraordinary power of erudition and this wealth of knowledge which Maryam was blessed with, which meant that a Prophet like Zakariyyah found himself confused and moved, to the point of questioning her on the origin of all this spiritual knowledge, he who was supposed to teach her and guide her:

> He would ask: 'O Mary, whence came this unto thee?'
> She would answer: 'It is from God; behold, God grants
> sustenance unto whom He wills, beyond all reckoning.'
> (Āl 'Imrān 3: 37)

Maryam, this creature in the prime of life, she who as a woman was

---

55. Rashid Rida, *Tafsīr al-Manar*, vol. 3, p. 242.
56. Sahl al-Tustari, *Tafsīr al-Qur'an al-'Azim*, in Mary, mother of Jesus, by Pierre Lory.

preordained for all except this rank of venerable sages, peacefully enlightened Zakariyyah on the origin of her knowledge. God gives to whom He wills without measure ... and God gave to Maryam without measure. Zakariyyah, God's Prophet, was stunned by her response ... There was such reassurance and such serenity emanating from her response that he, Prophet and spiritual master of this young believer, inculcated himself with this light and the knowledge of his young student!

This is what the Qur'an evokes in the subsequent art of the story:

> *In that self-same place* [mihrab], *Zachariah prayed unto his Sustainer, saying: 'O my Sustainer! Bestow upon me [too], out of Thy grace, the gift of goodly offspring; for Thou, indeed, hearest all prayer.'* (Āl 'Imrān 3: 38)

It is as if Maryam's experience revived in Zakariyyah's heart the remembrance of God ... He realized, in contemplating Maryam, the strength of Divine power and its capacity to give without limits to His faithful believers ... Maryam's mystical fervour incited her to do the same. And as in his late age he was without children, he implored his Creator, Capable of all wonders, to fulfil him with a virtuous progeny similar to that which he had before his eyes. He went to pray like her in the same *mihrab*, and like her, he invoked He who 'gives without measure'!

Revelation and annunciation
It is thus isolated in her place of retreat that Maryam dedicated herself to meditation and daily spiritual renewal and it is in this same *mihrab* that she received first a Divine revelation of *guidance*, followed thereafter by the *annunciation* by the archangel Gabriel of the birth of the future Messiah.

Withdrawn in this *mihrab*, which according to al-Qurṭubi designates the most elevated place of any sacred space, Maryam initially received angels who informed her of her *predilection* by God the Almighty.

> *AND LO! The angels said: "O Mary! Behold, God has*
> *elected thee and made thee pure, and raised thee above*
> *all the women of the world. O Mary! Remain thou truly*
> *devout unto thy Sustainer, and prostrate thyself in worship,*
> *and bow down with those who bow down [before Him]."*
> (*Āl 'Imrān* 3: 42–43)

It is vital to note here that the angels call on Maryam by her own name, which as we have previously evoked, seems to translate the extent of closeness and intimacy of this woman with God ... She was without doubt *close* to God ... The beauty of this call must in itself suffice us in imagining the exceptionally privileged position which Maryam occupies by the Lord of the worlds!

God thus chose Maryam and purified her then He chose her a second time. This repetition is not a mere repetition in form but rather a spiritual confirmation ... The first selection seems to be that of dignity, of the eminent position and the purification from all sins and transgressions, through Divine grace, whereas the second appears to be the birth of Prophet 'Isa, in which no woman in the world resembles her nor will resemble her until Resurrection day.[57]

This predestination of Maryam, her purity and her highly privileged spiritual position are also related in narrations of Prophet Muhammad which confirm the pre-eminence afforded to Maryam. According to the Prophet of Islam, there are four best women in the world: Maryam bint 'Imran, Asiah the wife of Pharaoh, Khadija bint Khuwaylid and Fatima daughter of the Messenger of God.[58] The Divine protection of Maryam is outlined in another hadith: 'There is none born among the offspring of Adam, but Satan touches it. A child therefore, cries loudly at the time of birth because of the touch of Satan, except Mary and her child.'[59]

After the angels confirmed to Maryam that she was chosen

---

57. *Tafsīr* of al-Qushayri, *Lata'if al-Isharat*, vol. 1 (Beirut: Dar al-Kutub al-'Ilmiyya, 2001).
58. Hadith reported by Anas Ibn Malik.
59. Hadith transmitted by Abu Hurayra.

by God, they recommended that she reinforce and consolidate her fervour and piety by seeking refuge, every day a little more, in contemplation and meditation. It is as if God wanted to prepare her for the great future challenge which lay ahead by reinforcing her faith, forging her personality and supplying her with all the spiritual energy necessary in order to confront her unique destiny.

God exhorted her to be one of his worshippers and His chosen ones and to excel in her devotion in order that she might become the spiritual receptacle for this great event, known to humanity, as the miraculous birth of 'Isa, the great Messiah ... .

Day after day, Maryam was preparing herself without knowing for the great day in her life. She was submitting to God each day a little more deeply, she was scrupulously following the Divine injunctions and, thus, extending her stays in the temple, whole days and nights, praying, meditating, recharging herself in His light, preciously preserving the spiritual treasure that God had generously offered, until the moment where the great revelation occurred: that of the annunciation.

This is what the Qur'an reveals in one of its verses:

> AND CALL to mind, through this Divine writ, Mary.
> Lo! She withdrew from her family to an eastern place
> and kept herself in seclusion [hijaban] from them [...].
> (Maryam 19: 16–17)

The classical exegeses do not linger on the interpretation of this verse where there is a reference to the even greater isolation of Maryam, in an oriental corner, withdrawn from her people behind a veil. Nonetheless, one can rightfully ask what the deep significance is of this 'oriental' retreat by Maryam and this mysterious 'veil' between her and her people.

Mystical commentators are more eloquent and seek to pierce 'the veils' of this solitude of Maryam's in order to find within it a symbolic attitude laden with meaning. This is how certain sufi scholars interpret Maryam's oriental isolation as her detachment from the natural world, from the carnal soul and its faculties. She has, according to their explanations, rejoined the Orient of the sacred world, the location of the Holy Ghost, which represents precisely the condition necessary for the reception of the Divine verb.[60] The 'veil' in question is the sacred enclosure, the protected location of the heart, inaccessible to what belongs to the world of the carnal heart or *nafs*. The Holy Ghost finds its access within it, if the space is truly *stripped*, as was Maryam's heart, entirely dedicated to her Creator.[61]

It was thus *initiated* in this fashion, in a profound state of abnegation, seemingly very vulnerable for those seeing her outward humility, but terribly strong in her inner-self through Divine favour, that she received an unexpected visitor, a strange visitor coming on behalf of his Creator.

In the following verse, the annunciation reaches the height of spiritual revelation:

> [A]nd kept herself in seclusion from them, whereupon
> We sent unto her Our angel of revelation, who appeared
> to her in the shape of a well-made human being. She
> exclaimed: "Verily, I seek refuge from thee with the Most
> Gracious! [Approach me not] if thou art conscious of Him!"
> [The angel] answered: 'I am but a messenger of thy
> Sustainer, [who says,] 'I shall bestow upon thee the gift of a
> son endowed with purity.' Said she: "How can I have a son
> when no man has ever touched me? – for, never have I been
> a loose woman!" [The angel] answered: 'Thus it is; [but]
> thy Sustainer says, 'This is easy for Me; and [thou shalt have
> a son,] so that We might make him a symbol unto mankind
> and an act of grace from US [...].'" (Maryam 19: 17–21)

Apparently Maryam was rather used to visits from angels in their immaterial form given that when she is visited by the angel Jibril in full human form, as outlined by the Qur'an, she was initially *appalled* by his sudden presence in a private sacred space. Her

---

60. Sahl al-Tustari, *Tafsīr al-Qur'ān al-'Azim*, cited in *Mary, mother of Jesus* Pierre Lory.

61. Qāshani Abderrazak, *Tafsīr Ibn 'Arabi*, cited in Lory, Ibid.

first reaction was to *defend* herself verbally by calling on Divine protection and by warning him against any ill will towards her. The angel sought to reassure her by announcing *the news* of the future birth of Prophet 'Isa.

Relieved to find himself faced with a messenger from her Creator, and the initial fear overcome, she found herself facing this serious and alarming revelation: *she would become pregnant with a Prophet child*! One can imagine the feelings of worry and fear experienced at that moment by this devout young woman who was far from thinking that God would task her with such a great responsibility!

In this profound moment of loneliness, she found herself faced with a messenger of God who came to transmit this secret eternally prescribed in the great book of human destiny ... A great secret, perhaps one of the greatest secrets that any human being on earth has ever received! A secret between herself and God who had chosen her, Maryam, to give birth through the grace of God a new messenger to humanity! Such news must surely have thrown her initially, but despite being overcome with emotion, she still felt able to question God's messenger and to debate with him concerning the logic of this undertaking ... *'How can I have a son when no man has ever touched me? – for, never have I been a loose woman!'* she asks.

The collective and popularized image of a devout, pious and submitted Maryam is often associated with a retiring, shy, even naïve woman. And yet the Qur'anic story, for those undertaking a profound reading, reveals a rather novel facet of this woman, namely that of her intelligence and her capacity for discernment. In fact, whilst convinced of the content of the message and its objective, she had the intellectual courage and the good sense to question the angel Jibril on the wherefore of this procreation which appeared to her, rightly so, entirely contrary to expectation. She was not intimidated either by the isolation with this man, nor by the spiritual intensity of the moment. She who was initiated from her young age in the purification of the spirit and body, who was conscious of the gravity of the moment she was experiencing and the importance of the messenger who was before her, she could have been satisfied from the beginning that he was a messenger of

God! Her deep faith and all her prior spiritual preparation did not impede her from using her reason to question her interlocutor, to reflect and try to understand.

The angel Jibril gives her an answer transmitted by God: '*Such was decided by your Lord.*' Such a solemn answer which informs her of the irrevocability of such an act prescribed in her destiny ... .

Human reason has its limitations in the face of the supreme Divine will of the Creator of this world and Maryam, sustained by this Divine knowledge, resigned herself to carry this heavy burden which the Lord had assigned to her. She had no choice, she was chosen by God and God's chosen people are those who experience the most arduous of trials. It is with these confused feelings, of happiness and fear, of doubt and uncertainty that she submitted to the Divine decree. All the while knowing that she was beloved by God, His favourite also, she could nonetheless not cease to feel a deep apprehension in her inner self and a real fear faced with the magnitude of the future and heavy responsibility which lay ahead.

The birth of 'Isa and all the struggles

In the subsequent Qur'anic verses we find a pregnant Maryam confronted with the pain of childbirth. The Qur'anic narrative ignores her pregnancy but describes in infinite beauty the scene of childbirth in which Maryam, desperately alone, struggles between pain, fear and helplessness while giving birth to this miraculous baby:

> *And in time she conceived him, and then she withdrew with him to a far-off place. And [when] the throes of childbirth drove her to the trunk of a palm-tree, she exclaimed: "Oh, would that I had died ere this, and had become a thing forgotten, utterly forgotten!"* (Maryam 19: 22–23)

One perceives through this verse Maryam's cry of despair as she, in the depths of the physical pains of her delivery, she wished to be dead and buried. She preferred to be forever forgotten than to experience this superhuman struggle. This moment of distress proves the extent to which the impact of this birth on Maryam's conscience must have been extremely difficult, despite the intense prior spiritual preparation and the Divine protection from which she benefited ... .

The Qur'an initially relates her isolation, pregnant, in a far-away place, which illustrates already her state of being and her desire to escape from people. Maryam, still condemned to living withdrawn from others ... Whereas in the beginning she isolated herself from others in order to better experience her relationship to God, in these circumstances she distanced herself through fear of other people's judgement, of their potential accusations, of their gossiping ... .

The struggle, one can easily imagine, was far from being humanly bearable and is subtly translated by the Qur'anic image of the dried palm trunk, the only companion of this abandoned soul. It is thus on this poor, dried up tree trunk that she went to lean on, in an ultimate gesture of distress, in order to briefly alleviate the pains which were tormenting her ... .

She also could not help but tragically apprehend the future arrival of this child, fruit of her womb certainly, but who would apparently turn her whole life upside down. Despite her submission to the Divine will and her trust in God, fear of judgement from others terrorized her and the darkest thoughts haunted her mind. How could she confront others, her family, the individuals from her community, all of them so proud of her? How could they believe in the birth of a child without a father? How could she convince them? How would she withstand their accusations, their suspicions, their distrust towards her? At that precise moment, she wished to be hidden beneath the earth, forgotten, disappeared, dead for good, rather than to live through the attack on her honour ... She, the virtuous, who dedicated all her time to the worship of the Creator, she who was admired for her piety, her devotion and her chastity! Who would think she would one day have to live through such accusations?

These are thoughts which were constantly going through Maryam's mind as she gave birth in pain (emotional and physical) ... It is at that moment that a voice was heard ... a voice which came to appease her and comfort her in her pain, her sadness and her immeasurable helplessness ... .

> *Thereupon [a voice] called out to her from beneath that [palm-tree]: "Grieve not! Thy Sustainer has provided a rivulet [running] beneath thee and shake the trunk of the palm-tree towards thee: it will drop fresh, ripe dates upon thee. Eat, then, and drink, and let thine eye be gladdened! And if thou shouldst see any human being, convey this unto him: Behold, abstinence from speech have I vowed unto the Most Gracious; hence, I may not speak today to any mortal.'"*
> (*Maryam* 19: 24-26)

The classical exegeses diverge in their views on the origin of this voice. Some state that it was the angel Jibril, whereas others claim instead that it was 'Isa, still a newborn, who spoke to his mother.[62] Whatever the provenance of this voice, what is important here is that in both cases, whether it was the angel or 'Isa, it was Divine clemency which was manifesting itself through them in all its splendour.

Whereas Maryam appeared to perish, in a state of profound distress and severe suffering, the Creator came to her rescue with His most beautiful words. He transmitted a message of consolation and appeasement to her and alleviated her pain and sadness with His words full of gentleness and serenity ... God provided her with all that she needed, water from the stream which ran by her feet, fresh dates from the dead palm tree but which was revived to satisfy her hunger ... She was no longer alone! He was there, by her side, taking care of her every need, soothing her body and soul: 'Stop crying!' the Lord of the world was telling her. How much beauty and light can be found in this Divine consolation! God encouraged her to be glad in that moment, admittedly hard, but only temporary ... 'Stop crying!' because what awaits you, Maryam, as a reward will be infinitely greater! That's what the mysterious voice was telling her ... .

---

62. *Tafsir* of Tabari.

Maryam and her son, a 'sign' for the worlds
While comforting her, God seemed to be preparing Maryam psychologically for the coming challenge, the one that which she was most apprehensive about: the confrontation with her people!

He guided her slowly, exhorting her not to speak to people she encountered, in order words, he advised her to mark a fasting of speech.

To face the others, she had to maintain her silence, a silence of words, which is testimony to this wonderful Divine approach and which substitutes speech for the silent attitude of human dignity ... The moment was serious and Maryam promised to undertake a great fast of speech, she had to remain dignified. The majority of scholars agree that this promise of a fast of words was a sign or, *ayah* exclusive to Maryam and her child, none can pretend to this fast of words after her.[63]

The mystical interpretation has long commentaries on Maryam's speech fast. According to some, it was a case of fasting from everything, save from the remembrance of God. Maryam had to find solace in God and rest her heart in Him, hence the instruction not to speak to another human being.[64] Others think the silence represents the abandoning of recourse to one's self (*nafs*): 'If you wanted to speak to plead your innocence yourself, he says through Mariam, you would only increase the difficulty, whereas your silence allows us to manifest our omnipotence.'[65]

One of the classical commentators interprets this silence as the best answer Maryam could give to her people, because no response or justification could convince them of the veracity of these facts.[66]

In fact, her people, seeing her arrive with a baby in her arms, were profoundly consternated and immediately showered her with offensive accusations. The Qur'an conveys some of this slander:

---

63. Ibid.
64. *Tafsīr* of Tustari.
65. Lory, in *Mary, mother of Jesus*.
66. *Tafsīr* of Tabari.

> *And in time she returned to her people, carrying the child with*
> *her. They said: "O Mary! Thou hast indeed done an amazing*
> *thing! O sister of Aaron! Thy father was not a wicked man,*
> *nor was thy mother a loose woman!" Thereupon she pointed*
> *to him. They exclaimed: "How can we talk to one who*
> *[as yet] is a little boy in the cradle?" [But] he said: 'Behold, I*
> *am a servant of God. He has vouchsafed unto me revelation*
> *and made me a Prophet. (Maryam 19: 27–30)*

Her people, despite being witnesses to her past as a pious young woman, virtuous and entirely devoted to her Creator, were not understanding toward her, not even out of consideration for that not so distant past ... All the admiration she had been afforded as well as the respect she was entitled to vanished and gave way to an animosity and virulent hostility. Instead of demonstrating kindness and caution, if only with regards to her exemplary past, they rapidly succumbed to defamation, incriminating her through their diatribes, while Maryam remained dignified in her silence.

She endured, serene, patient, in the face of all their criticism ... Once aware of her role as heiress of the great secret, the very secret which linked her to her Lord, now she knew herself to be protected, guided and loved to that extent by God, nothing else was of importance.

Maryam thus remained silent despite her people incessantly condemning her and it was at that precise moment that God made 'Isa her child speak in order to clear her name, she who had kept the Divine secret ... 'Isa's speech, still a baby in his crib, was a decisive argument which sufficed in itself to rehabilitate Maryam in the eyes of her community. The sufi exegesis suggests that 'Isa at this stage symbolized Maryam's inner dimension, the two in fact constituted a single unit. Does the Qur'an itself not highlight on two occasions that Isa and his mother represent a single and same 'sign' (ayah)?

> *We made the son of Mary and his mother a symbol [of Our*
> *grace][...]. (al-Mu'minūn 23: 50)*

And in another verse:

> AND [remember] her who guarded her chastity, whereupon
> We breathed into her of Our spirit and caused her, together
> with her son, to become a symbol [of Our grace] [...].
> (al-Anbiyā' 21: 91)

Maryam is certainly a 'sign' for the universe and it is worth
emphasising here the importance of this term in the Qur'an, in
which it is always used to describe the marvels of Divine creation.
It is important to underline here that, despite the miraculous birth
of 'Isa, the Qur'an repeats on several occasions that he was only a
Prophet like others, human first and foremost and son of a saintly
woman chosen by God, but nonetheless, one who was humbly
human:

> The Christ, son of Mary, was but an apostle: all [other]
> apostles had passed away before him; and his mother was one
> who never deviated from the truth; and they both ate food
> [like other mortals] [...]. (al-Mā'ida 5: 75)

Maryam, chosen by God, His favourite ... she will remain for eternity,
as decreed by the Qur'an, the undeniable testimony to beautiful
feminine spirituality, brilliantly emanating light and truth but also
so human ... .

Here ends the story of Maryam as it is described in the Qur'an
and begins that of her son whom God evokes more often under the
designation 'son of Maryam', he who draws his legitimate filiations
from her and her alone! This is how the story of this Prophet beloved
of God continues in the Qur'an, under this name 'Isa *ibn Maryam*,
as if to remind us of her, incessantly, inevitably, even through her
son and by her son ... In order that we never forget that this great
Prophet was first and foremost the son of Maryam ... .

PART TWO

WHEN THE QUR'AN SPEAKS TO WOMEN

The language of the Qur'an, a masculine language?
We've seen how the Qur'an speaks about women, through the examples of illustrious female characters, depicted with great subtleness, beauty and eloquence.

Here, the Divine word comes to counter what social prejudice continues to support in the name of a universally accepted *sacrality*; that of the discrimination against women, structurally weaker beings, destined to subordination.

Through these Qur'anic stories about women, one perceives a constant desire to recognize and appreciate this consistently assailed feminine identity. Women as *vectors* of faith, which was a new conception of femininity and in particular the anticipated announcement of a project of liberation, replete with meaning, for the climate of the time.

It is especially important to bear in mind the framework of revelation, that of an intransigent patriarchal context where women were all but a human being worthy of dignity. It is at the heart of this Bedouin society with its very harsh mores, its implacably misogynistic ancestral customs and which ignores the feminine being, that the Qur'an reveals its feminine models of Muslim women, believing, intelligent. Qur'anic image of sovereign enlightened women, of saints, educators, scholars, resistors, passionate figures as we discover them through *Balkis*, Maryam, Asiah and all the others.

Beside this Divine speech talking *about* women, there is that which speaks *to* women, directly, personally and solemnly ... .

It is true that the Qur'an is the Divine word destined for all human beings regardless of their gender, their ethnicity or their colour, a speech which addresses human beings in what is most noble in their soul: their reason and their intellect.

Muslim scholars more or less agree that the *masculine* language expressed in the Qur'an systemically includes the *feminine gender* and that Divine words in general speak to both women and men, without any distinction.[1] The masculine gender in the Qur'an is used as a neutral gender and the formalisation of masculine language implies human universality. The term 'men' or, *rijal* in Arabic is polysemous and also signifies an elite of men and women. This linguistic characteristic is moreover not exclusive to the Arabic language as it is used in the Qur'an. All the other universal languages use masculine as a neutral gender. Does the term 'men' in English not also encompass *human beings* in general? This formalisation of the word *man* as a universal category is actually being questioned today. This is the case when it comes to the terminology used in the universal charter of *Human Rights* which many are currently seeking to reform.[2]

Nonetheless, the Qur'anic text uses the feminine gender in very precise circumstances and employs a strictly feminine language in this case, where the discourse involves calling on women specifically to respond to quests emanating from a given context or right an injustice committed against them. It is a Divine word which descends from the high Heavens specifically for them as if to better free them, better emancipate them from outdated customs, give them a new breath ... as if to better love them also.

---

1. Regarding equality in the Qur'anic discourse, it is affirmed by numerous scholars including the jurist Ibn Rushd, Imam Ibn al-Qayyim and Ibn 'Arabi. See, *Tahrir al-Mar'a fi 'Asr ar-Risala* by Abu Shuqqah, p. 70, in 'Arabic, 4th edition, (Kuwait: Dar al-Qalam edition, 1995).

2. Agnès Callamard, *Le sexism à fleur de mots*, *le Monde Diplomatique*, March 1998.

When the Qur'an responds to feminine demands

The study of the circumstances of the revelation of the Qur'an, often referred to as *asbab an-nuzul*, reveals the involvement of a certain number of women in the context of revelation in several Qur'anic verses. That is the case for example in the following verse:

> VERILY, for all men and women who have surrendered themselves unto God, and all believing men and believing women, and all truly devout men and truly devout women, and all men and women who are true to their word, and all men and women who are patient in adversity, and all men and women who humble themselves [before God], and all men and women who give in charity, and all self-denying men and self-denying women, and all men and women who are mindful of their chastity, and all men and women who remember God unceasingly: for [all of] them has God readied forgiveness of sins and a mighty reward. (al-Aḥzāb 33: 35)

Concerning the causes of the revelation of this verse, the exegetical commentaries report several versions which differ not in their meaning or content, but at the level of the individuals concerned. The most well-known interpretation is that reported, among others, by Tabari and which concerns Umm Salama, the wife of the Prophet. In fact, according to this version, Hind bint Abi Umayya, better known under the name Umm Salama, was reported to have once said to the Prophet: *'Why are we women not mentioned in the Qur'an as men are?'* The same day, during the *zuhur* prayer, the Prophet announced from the top of his *minbar*: 'Oh you all, this is what God says in His Qur'an ... .'[3]

Then he shared with them the revelation of the verse. According to another variation still by Umma Salama, she is said to have stated: *'Why are men mentioned on every occasion and not us women?'*[4]

Another version is that of Ibn 'Abbas who reports that it was the wives of the Prophet, without specifying which one in particular,

---

3. *Tafsīr* by Tabari, hadith reported by Ibn Shayba.
4. *Tafsīr* by Tabari, hadith by Mujahid.

who asked: 'Why does God mention the believing men and not the believing women?' Other exegetes attribute these words to other women in the Muslim community, outside of the wives of the Prophet, whereas others refer to Asma' bint Umays who once she'd returned from Abyssinia – today's Ethiopia – asked the wives of the Messenger if God had revealed something in their favour. She was seemingly referring to those who, like her, had emigrated from Makkah to this African region. Faced with the negative response from the wives of the Prophet, she went to find him and said: *'We women are truly saddened by what is happening to us!'* And the Prophet is said to have responded: 'Why so?' – *'Because we are not referred to in the Qur'an in the same way that men are!'* she responded to him.[5]

A final relatively well known version, is that which attributes the women's demands to Umm 'Umarah al-Ansariyya who is said to have stated to the Prophet: *'I see that everything is in favour of men and that women are not even referenced by the Divine words!'*[6]

Notwithstanding the divergence of scholars concerning the author of this feminine demand, it nonetheless remains clear that the content remains the same. It is women who demonstrated their great dissatisfaction to the Prophet faced with a Qur'anic discourse which seemed – to their eyes – to ignore them! What is more, given the diverse sources which exist concerning this story, it seems entirely likely that there were several of them who expressed the same resentment ... .

This behaviour is in itself very revealing of the state of mind of the Muslim women of the time who felt so committed to this *path* of faith, as much as the men if not more, that they did not hesitate to demand a commitment to greater equality on the part of the Creator.

They wanted an equality transcribed in the sacred text for eternity, and this, despite the fact they must have known pertinently well that the Qur'anic discourse, through its neutral masculine tone, referred to them as much as it did to men. Nonetheless, and as if they felt wronged at a particular moment in the narrative, they

---

5. *Tafsīr* of al-Baghawi, hadith by Muqatil.
6. *Tafsīr* of al-Qurṭubi, hadith reported by Tirmidhi.

wished to express their disappointment openly and publicly, with the precise aim of reaffirming their position of equality.

This is well and truly a feminist demand ... demanding rights similar to those of men, and was the beginning of a new feminine conscience which was not content with simply being assimilated into a general concept of believer but which demanded a distinct recognition in good and due form.

One can only marvel at the *bravery* of these women who did not hesitate to demand the same recognition as that naturally afforded to men, to the Prophet of Islam, a request conveyed, it is worth noting, under the form of an official critique. These women, who must have been spiritually blossoming, in order to express themselves in this fashion, were clearly questioning the revelation.

They were acting in this fashion simply because it was this same revelation which introduced them to freedom of expression ...

It was this same revelation which taught them that they were human beings born free and that no other submission would be accepted in Islam than that owed to the Creator. It is this same revelation which taught them to behave as responsible and autonomous human beings ... Beings free to manifest their reprobation, to protest, to demand in the name of faith. It was in the name of all of this that they *criticized* what appeared to them as a somewhat *masculine* connotation of the sacred text, a reproach which stemmed from their profound conviction in Divine justice!

Could we imagine such a scenario in our contemporary Muslim societies without there being an outcry of protests or worse, an inflamed indictment? Yes today, when the mere fact of debating religious matters is looked down on and where questioning even Islamic interpretations is considered sacrilegious. Discussions are rejected despite the fact no profound and intelligent understanding of the text can be acquired without a serene, critical and constructive debate. Formulating questions in the face of the complexity of religious discourse is legitimate and debating them can only reinforce convictions which, although established, remain very vulnerable!

This is what these early believing women aspired to, in expressing their critique. They wanted an answer which, while *reinforcing* their real position within a community very marked by the prevailing patriarchal culture, would reinforce their convictions and alleviate their heart. What could be more legitimate for these women who, at the dawn of Islam, were in full *conquest* of their rights, than to affirm their presence by *demanding* clear answers concerning their spiritual equality? And how today, faced with a discriminatory interpretation of the religious sphere, can we deny women this same right, namely that of having a critical eye concerning the manifest dysfunctionalities in the reading of scriptural texts?

Faced with this veritable *grievance* from the women of his community, the Prophet had no particular response. Rather he stayed quiet, a sympathetic silence. Was he not the one who always demonstrated sensitivity and understanding faced with the suffering of women?

But the answer didn't take long to *come down* and God *responded* to the demands of these women ... The verse which was revealed following this feminine demand illustrates indisputably that these women's questioning was legitimate!

The content of the verse testifies to this Divine Will to realize the desire of Muslim women to see themselves solemnly mentioned, to know themselves to be honoured and eternally recognized. God explicitly distinguishes in this verse between the two genders in order to highlight His egalitarian vision. '*The Muslim men and the Muslim women, the believing men and the believing women [...] those, male and female [...] God has reserved [...] a magnificent reward.*' It is this Divine response, incredibly beautiful, which requires no commentary – which we must always have in mind, which we must know how to re-read and re-interpret every time we have a doubt concerning the egalitarian spirit of the message of Islam. Every time we are assailed by the perpetual intellectual aggressions on Islam and women ... Every time that our hearts, as women and men, want to be appeased ... Each time we want to evaluate our reality as Muslims to that of the Qur'an.

> *[T]hose who believe, and whose hearts find their rest in the*
> *remembrance of God – for, verily, in the remembrance of*
> *God [men's] hearts do find their rest. (al Ra'd 13: 28)*

Among the other Qur'anic verses through which God responds to women's expectations, is the verse which was revealed after the wife of the Prophet, Umm Salama's protest concerning the Hijrah or the exile of women.

In fact, Umm Salama expressed her profound regret at the Qur'an's silence concerning the participation of women in the expatriation of Hijrah, which was a primordial stage in the story of Islam.

The tradition states that Umm Salama told the Messenger: 'Men are mentioned in the Qur'an several times for their participation in the Hijrah whereas we women, are not mentioned at all!'[7] This was the basis for the revelation of the following verse:

> *And thus does their Sustainer answer their prayer: "I shall*
> *not lose sight of the labour of any of you who labours [in*
> *My way], be it man or woman: each of you is an issue of*
> *the other. Hence, as for those who forsake the domain of evil,*
> *and are driven from their homelands, and suffer hurt in My*
> *cause, and fight [for it], and are slain – I shall most certainly*
> *efface their bad deeds, and shall most certainly bring them*
> *into gardens through which running waters flow, as a reward*
> *from God: for with God is the most beauteous of rewards."*
> *(Āl 'Imrān 3: 195)*

The Qur'anic exegeses state here that these verses were revealed immediately after the spirited protest by Umm Salama, which firstly confirms the high rank afforded to this woman by God, but also the importance of this expatriation of women as a political act in the Qur'anic vision.

---

7. Basis for the revelation of verse 195 of Surah Āl 'Imran, in the respective *tafsīr* of Tabari and Ibn Kathir, according to the version reported by Mujahīd.

Umm Salama's demands were doubly understandable for those whom the tradition nicknames '*the woman of two exiles*' due to her emigration on two occasions in Abyssinia. History reports that she was the first woman to emigrate from Makkah to Abyssinia with her first husband Abu Salama. This first forced exile came to be necessary after the abuses experienced by this couple both from the ruling Makkan elite and from within their own tribe.

Umm Salama has long accounts of the various events experienced while living in exile, on the suffering experienced by her and her different companies at the time and also during her emigration towards Madinah. In fact, the tradition relates the consecutive struggles she was forced to endure, especially when she was separated, against her will, from her husband and her child, by her own tribe and family. Separated from her spouse who, forced to leave her, heads to Madinah, and from her child taken by members of her family, she suffers an entire year, alone, inconsolable and spends whole days weeping for her child and husband ... .

Moved by the agony experienced by this woman, a notable from her family interceded with her tribe who returned her child to her and allowed her to rejoin her husband and the other Muslims in Madinah.

It was alone with her son, himself still a child, as her sole companion, that she undertook, despite the dangers she would face, the long exile to Madinah. She was resolute in heading to where her husband was in order that they might live their faith in peace together, in this new city of freedom which was the city of the Prophet. It was in a location a little outside Makkah that a valiant knight offered to accompany her to her destination.

It would be important perhaps to remind the reader at this stage that the person who offered his assistance and protection to this woman and her child was a non-Muslim and that this did not stop Umm Salama from accepting his help and subsequently praising his chivalrous attitude and his irreproachable moral conduct.[8]

There are in this short episode in Islamic history innumerable lessons to draw for our daily life as Muslims, where intolerance, even rejection of the other, have become a rule for some, as well as the twisted *mistrust* towards any company deemed *illicit* for a woman alone. Umm Salama was a woman without hang-ups, free and determined. Her faith, coupled with her virtuous behaviour, were amply sufficient to *protect* her as a *single* woman from any immoral attacks.

Faced with this trajectory of a resistor, in the true sense of the term, and of all the difficulties endured along these successive events, who could be surprised with the pertinence of Umm Salama's demands of the Prophet of Islam?

In her own name, but also in the name of those who, like her, had suffered so much during the various periods of exile, Umm Salama was merely expressing a sincere emotion, of sadness and disappointment in the face of the Qur'an's apparent silence concerning the boundless commitment of women in an act as important, politically speaking, as the Hijrah.

Only men appear to be rewarded for their contribution and no regard for those who, like Umm Salama and so many others, almost lost their lives and those of their children in order to protect their faith and their convictions ... .

But God is the Just and despite the fact His Divine words are intended to address all humans, women and men, He answered Umm Salama's call and clarified once again that women and men are fundamentally equal in their spiritual and political commitment.

'*I would never make any being, male or female, lose the outcome of their works because you come from one another*' (*ba'dukum min ba'd*). This is God's response to Umm Salama, revealed under the form of an eternal Divine promise which transcends time and history.

The promise to never allow the benefits acquired by some to be lost by others ... The promise to ensure that His Divine equity

---

8. The knight was 'Uthman ibn Abi Talha; see Amina Ameziane el Hassani, *Umm Salama Umm al-Mu'minin*, 1st Part one, (Morocco: Ministry of Habous and Islamic Affairs).

is always infinitely present, independently of gender, whatever the circumstances and the act allotted ... God, through His profound generosity, reassured her heart and that of all other women and *insisted* in this verse on the perfect equality between the sexes.

In fact, a classical commentator asserts that the expression 'to none of you, male or female' followed by '*you are drawn from one another*' expresses a desire to insist on God's part on reinforcing this notion of equality of women and men, by using this image of men and women '*linked to one another*' (*ba'dukum min ba'd*).[9]

It goes without saying that this verse testifies to the intensity of this union which should *link* men and women to one another, naturally, and which thus reaffirms their common origin.

God reminds us here that there could be no differences between beings from the same act of creation, from the same origin! Other scholars argue that the verse is the equivalent of another:

> AND [as for] the believers, both men and women they are close unto one another (*ba'duhum awliya'u ba'd*): they [all] enjoin the doing of what is right and forbid the doing of what is wrong [...].[10]

The assertion of equality between the two sexes is present there with the same intensity. This mutual alliance which is in fact a *co-responsibility*, is the major argument which delineates the criteria of male-female relations as they are established in the Qur'anic vision.

This verse alone is the pivot upon which equality is formulated, since it summarizes the very essence of political action which is incumbent on societal actors, female and male.

To command the good and forbid evil is a central task which falls upon not only the political authority in place, but upon each Muslim, male and female.

Each of them must struggle against oppression, do their best to ensure social justice and ensure that communal wealth is redistributed equitably.

---

9. *Tafsir* al-Baydawi.
10. *Al-Tawba* 9: 71.

As long as society is faithful to this major principle in Islam, of commanding good and forbidding evil, it is considered a just society.

This Divine injunction which incites believers, male and female, to show solidarity towards one another in this major political action, is the central proof that the Qur'anic vision is an indisputably egalitarian vision.

Nonetheless, it is distressing to see how certain classical exegeses are in total opposition with the Qur'anic conception of harmony, union and equality between women and men.

A certain number of scholars, prisoners of their respective cultural contexts, will be incapable of interpreting these sorts of verses other than according to a traditional and archaic outlook, and this, despite the fact that they may have more or less accepted a certain spiritual equality, constantly reiterated by the sacred text.

They avoid this egalitarian image of the Qur'an, despite clear verses, and end up *constraining* the text, by attributing discriminatory and derogatory connotations to it.

This misogynistic interpretation, transmitted to generations of Muslims, themselves locked into a conformist reading, ends up substituting itself to the Qur'anic message and becoming an immutable Islamic principle.

Al-mubahalah, or when the Qur'an encourages women social participation

In a verse of *surah Āl 'Imrān*, also known under the name of 'the scene of the *mubahalah*', God calls on his Prophet as follows:

> And if anyone should argue with thee about this [truth] after all the knowledge that has come unto thee, say: "Come! Let us summon our sons and your sons, and our women and your women, and ourselves and yourselves; and then let us pray [together] humbly and ardently, and let us invoke God's curse upon those [of us] who are telling a lie."
> (*Āl 'Imrān* 3: 61)

This verse was revealed on the occasion of the arrival in Madinah of a delegation of Christians from the tribe of Najran, with the intention of speaking with the Prophet.

He received them in his mosque in Madinah and the tradition reports that he authorized them to undertake their ritual prayers within the mosque itself.[11]

The religious high dignitaries of the Christian delegation began a purely theological discussion with the Prophet on a number of questions, of which very controversially were that of the *divinity* of 'Isa or that concerning the concept of the Trinity. Faced with the polemic tone of certain affirmations and the insistence of certain Christians who seemed to corner the Prophet to respond categorically to their interrogations, God *revealed* this verse in which He seems to encourage the Prophet to organize a sort of public assembly, to which the members of both Muslim and Christian communities should be invited.

The Prophet suggested to them therefore, and in conformity with the Divine order, to draw on the *mubahalah*, a sort of verbal confrontation, also known under the name *ordalie*.[12] It was in fact an ancient custom in which the two belligerent parties had to turn around face to face for a verbal duel, each raising their allegations on their side, while invoking Divine justice which alone can settle in favour of one of the two parties.

Hence, on the day of the meeting fixed with the group of Christians, the Prophet presented himself with the members of his family, including his two grandsons al-Hasan and al-Husain, his daughter Fatima Zahra and his son-in-law 'Ali.

The historical chronicles report that the Christian delegation ended up cancelling the visit, through fear of a potential Divine curse, but also out of fear of the consequences of a defeat on the morale of their co-religionists. The Christian religious chiefs then

---

11. *Tafsir* of Tabari.
12. The ordalies were in use during the second millennium BC until the twentieth century in Brittany (France) or in Africa. In the Middle Ages, they were known under the name *God's judgements* and have with time become a sort of *judicial challenge* or *judicial duel*, the outcome of which establishes the culpability or innocence of the accused.

proposed to the Prophet to seal a pact of peace and friendship with the Muslims, which the Prophet accepted, proving once again that Islam is first and foremost a religion which promotes co-existence with other religions of the Book in the respect and preservation of good relations.

Beyond the innumerable teachings which can be deduced from this historical episode, such as the Prophet's high level of consideration for those whom the Islamic tradition refers to as the 'people of the book', his respectful silence faced with their polemical altercations, his ability to accept the other whatever their beliefs, there is also this call from God to all His faithful, male and female, to participate as a believer in all social events, whatever their importance.

In this verse, there is a clear message from the Creator who encourages women – Muslim and non-Muslim – to contribute to public debates. There is here a veritable Divine will to ensure the participation and collaboration of women in all social projects, and this, in the same way as men.

It is clear in the higher objectives of the Qur'anic vision, called *maqasid as-Shari'ah*, this determination to include women at all levels of social participation.

This occurrence of the *mubahalah*, which occurred in a public space, was considered at the time in some ways as an opportunity to reveal the Truth, by using methods which were certainly imprecatory – such as the curse which was said to fall on those who propagated lies – but which were at the time the best method to *evaluate* people's good will.

Adapted to our context, we might imagine it as a sort of constructive dialogue or meeting between two opposing parties in which each would submit their arguments before a magistrate who alone could judge.

God wanted women to participate in these sorts of public debates, and the Prophet immediately responded to the call by ensuring the participation of she who would represent the women of his family, namely his beloved daughter Fatima Zahra.

The Prophet was merely submitting to the Divine injunction which required him to go, with all the members of his community – children, women and men – to this public meeting.[C] He started by setting the example himself by attending the event, accompanied by a representative of each of the members of his family.

Neither the exegesis nor the history of the narration provide further details on the subject such as knowing whether the other members of the Muslim community attended the meeting or whether there were other women aside from the daughter of the Prophet.[D] It is certainly true that the opposing side's decision to cancel the event did not allow for an estimation of the possible female participation from among the other women in the Muslim community, which certainly would have been important.

In any case, the example of the Prophet alone is in this sense edifying and informs us of the true place of women in a society which wishes to be *grounded* in the fundamental precepts of Islam. At a time when a very cautious religious vision is on offer, if not an entirely *static* one concerning women's social participation in all public debate – and this due to the alleged prohibition in Islam on so-called *'free-mix*ing', which has become a veritable *spectre* in so called practising Muslim communities – one could rightly ask what type of free mixing is being referred to when the Prophet himself never ceased to include women in all social action, whatever the level of importance, and in the same rank as men. This is how he educated the believers and this was reflected in the behaviour of those close to him. Umm Salama, 'Mother of the Believers', one of the most erudite women of the time, narrates that one day, as her servant was brushing her hair, she heard the call of the Prophet from the height of his *minbar*: *'Ayyuhu an-nas'* or 'Oh you people!' She got up in order to join the audience, when her servant asserted that the call did not concern women! Umm Salama responded: *'But I am one of the people!'*[13]

Similarly, the story of another female 'resistor' from among the earliest generation, Asma' bint Abi Bakr, who was, at a certain point in Muslim history, the only moral and material support of

13. Transmitted by Muslim.

the Prophet, follows the same line. It relates how one day, due to the loud noise which reigned in the mosque in Madinah, she was unable to hear the end of the Prophet's sermon. She asked a man sat next to her what the remainder of his words had been.[14]

These sorts of hadith, like many others, illustrate how during the period of revelation there never was any sort of material or psychological barrier between the male and female believers. This is how the believer, male or female, perceives the message of Islam as a spiritual message which calls on their humanity first and foremost and this is how the Messenger of Islam sought to transmit it to his companions, male and female.

Islamic history is replete with stories which illustrate how the Muslim community at the time of the Prophet was a community of women and men and that they worked together and side by side for the good of all, without losing themselves in secondary considerations, because their faith was there to protect them and there was no need for *barricades* in order to avoid potential moral *slip-ups*![15]

How have we arrived today at the point of developing impulses for separation between the sexes in all social congregations in the name of Islam, and imagining extraordinary strategies to separate feminine and masculine spaces with the objective of proving that the social act in itself is *very Islamic*? We obsessively hold on to appearances, when what should actually be Islamic is our behaviour towards one another. Instead of wasting our energy in the elaboration of virtual obstacles, we should rather focus our thinking on *educating* these women and men on the true dimension of Muslim spirituality. This perspective which ensures that piety, in other words attachment to moral and ethical values, is the only criteria for evaluation of each of us. A dimension which in itself erases differences between the sexes and allows us to see the other as a mirror to our own humanity.

And what more beautiful example of Islamic *free-mixing*, than

---

14. Hadith of Asma' bint Abi Bakr, reported by al-Hafiz Ibn Hajjar in Bukhari.
15. See on this topic the excellent publication by 'Abd al-Halim Abu Shuqqah, *Encyclopédie de la femme en Islam*, (Paris: Editions Al-Qalam, 2000).

this incredible event which is the hajj, the pilgrimage to Makkah where men and women circumambulate together, side by side, around the Kaaba! Is this event alone not a poignant *reminder* of the egalitarian essence of Islam?

The *Muhajirat*/ūn, or the female political refugees

From the beginning of his mission, the Prophet and the first Muslims had to face a real persecution from the Makkan oligarchy, notably from that of the Quraysh clan.

It is true that the message of Islam broke unequivocally with the ancient social order founded on customs, mercantile interest and the exploitation of the most vulnerable.

The concept of the *unicity of God* proclaimed by the Messenger constituted a real danger for the Arabs of the time, both politically and economically, since it placed into question the hierarchy of the social system essentially founded on the veneration of idols such as power and money, as well as the traditional worship of the elders represented by the supremacy of tribal links.

The hundreds of statues displayed at the time around the Kaaba were not there with an essentially cultural aim. They represented, each according to their origin and symbolic dimension, the economic power of a neighbouring tribe, a sort of *exploitation* conceded by the wealthy Quraysh elite, in order to protect the flow of commercial exchanges between these same tribes and Makkah.

The beneficiaries of this power, ultimately concentrated in the hands of a few chiefs, understood very quickly that the message of Islam seriously threatened them, since it advocated the freeing from all dominating and oppressive systems through the commitment to the submission to the one Creator.

Power, money, aristocracy and tribal identity no longer had a hold on a being who, through his faith, was becoming aware of his autonomy as an individual and it is in this that Islam – as it was revealed at the heart of a city like Makkah, a prestigious junction for commercial routes and a fundamental multi-religious centre – was sensed to be a dangerous message.

This is how the leaders of the Quraysh, faced with the widening of the circle of believers, the growing critiques of the ruling system in place and the weakening of their power, organized a veritable campaign of repression against the first Muslims. A repression which went from an economic boycott to targeted assassinations, via various moral sanctions and physical abuses.

Seeing this persecution intensifying day by day, the Prophet saw himself forced initially to strongly *advise* his faithful,[16] particularly those whose lives were seriously threatened, to immigrate to Abyssinia, governed at the time by Negus, a fair and honest Christian, as described by the Prophet himself.

It was subsequently that the Prophet organized the gradual exile of the faithful towards the future Madinah, city of this nascent Islam.

The first wave of emigration to Abyssinia was voluntary and temporary, whereas the second, that of Madinah, was obligatory for all Muslims, and it was this exodus of Muslims outside of their land of origin which was labelled Hijrah. The term literally signifies emigration or exile and the Hijrah of the Prophet to Madinah marked the beginning of the Islamic era and the beginning of Muslim history. This Hijrah, beyond its literal significance, represents a real rupture with the era of Jāhiliyyah, of a world *without laws*, a world steeped in *ignorance* ... Ignorance of God, of His message, of His presence. In adhering to the spiritual dimension of Islam, the believer realizes the objective of his presence on earth, reflects on his future, on his death and his life beyond and refuses to submit to the dictates of others. Accomplishing the Hijrah at that moment in history was to refuse the pre-established order, it was to move towards freedom, it was also undertaking an act of faith and worship.

This is how during the two stages of this Hijrah, the Muslim men and women experienced a veritable expatriation, leaving

---

16. This recommendation by the Prophet to head to Christian lands is laden with meaning and illustrates, to those who need it, that the objective of the message of Islam is not to annihilate other religions, as some wish to believe, but rather to rehabilitate the essential notion of the common message which binds all these religions, namely that of universal justice.

behind them their household, all their belongings, sometimes their family, their place of birth; all of this with the sole noble objective of protecting their faith and their convictions.

This exile constituted a real transformation of the political order of the time and was determining for the diffusion, expansion and the success experienced by the message of Islam from then onwards. Women and men, all were affected by this political action which was the Hijrah and this is what the Qur'an highlights by mentioning exiled women specifically, or the Muhajirat.

In fact, the Qur'an speaks of Muhajirat, a term which, similarly to the male equivalent Muhajirat, refers to expatriated women or refugees who undertook this Hijrah. The Qur'an says:

> O YOU who have attained to faith! Whenever believing women come unto you, forsaking the domain of evil, examine them, [although only] God is fully aware of their faith [...].
> (al-Mumtaḥana 60: 10)

We, therefore, note that God fully recognizes women's status as Muhajirat, in other words of political exiles. Notwithstanding the context, the profile of the Muhajirat of the time can be readily compared to that of political refugees as it is known today in universal legislation. In fact, this status is afforded to anyone who experiences severe prejudice in their country of origin, or who fears they might, due to their race, religion, ethnicity or political opinions.

The Muhajirat of the time were undeniably real political refugees since they were – like the men – forced to leave their ancestral home. In the same way as the men, they were forced, due to their faith, to face gruelling struggles, experience the worst torture and resist all manner of assaults.

It would be too lengthy to relate all the historical testimonies of persecutions experienced by the early Muslim women and this among all social classes, from the wealthiest to the poorest through to the highest nobility amongst them. Innumerable tales affirm the extent to which the Muslim woman has endured in the name of her faith and how she experienced exactly the same forms of physical torture as men.[17]

Sumayya
It might be useful here, for the sake of reference, to recall that the first martyr of Islam, namely the first person who died under torture because of her faith, was a woman. Sumayya Umm 'Ammar was stabbed in her lower stomach by a spear at the hands of Abu Jahl, a famous Makkan notary and sworn enemy of the Prophet, and this, after making her suffer the worst torture.

This woman was one of the first seven converts to Islam. Despite coming from a modest social background, she was not afraid to proclaim her Islam, to announce her conversion loudly and proudly at a time when many other Muslims, men in this case, preferred to keep their beliefs quiet. A woman who, very humbly, did not want to renounce her convictions despite the physical abuse she had to endure, she as well as all the members of her family. Nothing could have changed her mind and she refused to renege, even verbally, as her son subsequently did whom the Prophet had recommended he *renounce* his Islamic identity faced with his inability to cope with the suffering from the torture which was inflicted upon him ... .

Sumayya refused to renege her Islam in order to save her life, reaffirming under torture her commitment until the end, until the spear of Abu Jahl ensured her silence. Physical endurance, a central criterion in the differences between men and women, sometimes loses all its value in front of examples such as this one, namely that of a psychological endurance which far outweighs the greatest physical capabilities.

The example of Sumayya is in itself deifying and testifies to the magnitude of women's political participation at the time and of their conception of the message of Islam which, for these sorts of women, symbolized first and foremost a full responsibility. A political responsibility which the Qur'an gives them, in addition to reiterating in several verses. The detailed story of these Muhajirat

---

17. See the names of the tortured women in Ziyadah, *Dawr al-Mar'a as-Siyasi*, p. 115, op. cit.

is numerously retold by the early books of Islamic history which relate their resistance, their courage and their sacrifice even if, one notes, subsequently their contribution would be marginalized and rarely highlighted.[18]

Zaynab

One can cite as an example of narratives on exile that of Zaynab, the daughter of the Prophet. During her journey towards Madinah, Zaynab was seriously wounded by a group of assailants coming from Makkah and miscarried her child due to the attack. She died soon after, in Madinah, following the consequent blood-loss brought on by the miscarriage.[19]

Umm Sharik

There is also the story of Umm Sharik, a woman from a tribe called Daws, who converted to Islam during a stay in Makkah. She undertook an extraordinary job of spreading the message of Islam during the first clandestine stage, by entering into the various homes of women notables in Makkah and in inviting them to embrace this new religion.

Her intense activity of proselytism was ultimately uncovered by the Quraysh who handed her over to the members of her tribe. The latter put her through innumerable abuses in order to force her to recant her beliefs.

She recounts herself in numerous stories how she was tortured, abandoned and tied up under the desert sun, without water for days on end, yet she refused to give in, and even during her most profound distress she raised her index finger in a sign of her belief in the One God. Her people ended up abandoning her and she wished only one thing, to join the Prophet and the other Muslims in Madinah!

The journey was long, dangerous and risky for a woman on her own. She spent a long time seeking out someone who could escort her to Madinah and she ended up getting the assistance of a Jewish

---

18. Full index of the, Muhajirat in, *At-Tabaqat al-Kubra* by Ibn Sa'd.
19. Tabari, *Tarikh*.

man who, saddened to see her in this way, volunteered his help and accompanied her to Madinah.[20] Once in Madinah, Umm Sharik, according to certain versions, personally proposed to the Prophet. The Qur'an in fact mentions this unusual gesture, all the while referring to her by the term believer (*mu'mina*):

> [...] any believing woman who offers herself freely to the Prophet. [...]. (al-Aḥzāb 33: 50)

This clearly very audacious behaviour, both for the time and in our current context, was not criticized by the Qur'an at all! On the contrary, the term 'believer' used in the Divine language is very rewarding and is testimony to the acceptance of an action which at the time, was strongly condemned, notably by Ā'ishah, the wife of the Prophet.[21]

One can read into this reference to a 'believer', a testimony to the Qur'an's recognition of the struggle undertaken by this woman in the name of her faith and the valorisation of a personal act, certainly a very *bold* one, which highlights the very strong personality of this Muslim woman from the early generation. She who, convinced from the start by the message of Islam, initiated an exemplary path, that of one of the first clandestine female Muslim campaigners, who was respectively a prisoner, tortured for her offending opinions, then a political refugee.

It is this female profile, with a strong personality, blossoming, sincere and of a great bravery that the Qur'an evokes, and not that of an inevitably oppressed, retiring woman and an eternal victim: the implacable stereotype of the Muslim woman today!

---

20. Reported by Abu Hurayra from the narration of Yūnus ibn Bakir. The story in detail is taken from Muḥammad Saʾid Mabid, *Mawsu'at Hayat as-Sahabiyat*, al-Ghazali editions, Syria, 2000, p. 144.
21. Narrative by Umm Sharik and of the criticism made by Ā'ishah in Muḥammad Saʾid Mabid *Mawsu'at Hayat*, listed in, *at-Tabaqat al-Kubra* by Ibn Saʾd.

Asma' bint Abi Bakr

Another example is that of the famous Asma' bint Abi Bakr who also had an impressive trajectory and whose crucial role during the early days of the revelation is very telling. Was she not the one who kept secret the planned date for the Prophet and her own father Abi Bakr's departure towards Madinah, both of whom were under strict surveillance from their enemies the Quraysh?

The latter, with at their head the same Abu Jahl, came to persecute Asma', while looking for the Prophet, and in the face of her unmovable silence she received a slap at the hand of Abu Jahl, who was exasperated by her impassiveness. She was also the one who secretly ensured the subsistence of the Prophet, accompanied by Abu Bakr, during their sojourn in the cave on their path to exile. In fact, the Prophet nicknamed Asma' *dhat an-nitaqayn*, in other words she 'of the two belts', due to the fact she was concealing the provisions she was transporting for the Prophet and her own father, Abu Bakr as-Siddiq, on either side of her waist thanks to the two belts.

Asma' bint Abi Bakr was predicted to Paradise as a *mubashsharah bil janna*[22] by the Prophet and this is testimony to the extent of her action in the Hijrah. She was the only person to have protected, helped and supported the Prophet during his departure for Madinah, the future city of Islam. She fully participated in an immeasurable way to a decisive moment in the history of revelation, namely that of the management and organisation of the exile of the Prophet, an exile which, it should be remembered, was a determining stage for the future of the Prophetic mission.

And the others ...

Sumayya, the first martyr of Islam, Zaynab, daughter of the Prophet who, while pregnant, took the risk of going into exile and suffered a fatal attack on the way; Umm Sharik, who was persecuted and imprisoned then set out on a journey of exile accompanied by a well-intentioned Jewish man; Asma, she who alone organized in secret the exile of the Prophet; without forgetting Umm Salama

---

22. Muḥammad Sa'id Mabid, *Mawsu'at Hayat.*

who, as we have already stated, decided to set out alone into exile and was ultimately accompanied part of the way by a non-believer ...

All these examples, among many others, of persecuted women; humiliated, tortured and exiled, are they not indisputable examples of the importance of the participation of Muslim women in this stage of the Hijrah or political exile?

None can contest that it was thanks to this Hijrah of women that the first city of Islam was constructed. These examples and so many others are testimony to the intense political effervescence of the time and of the efficiency of female participation. They were always present, as much during the clandestine spread of the message as in the torture camps, or in the organisation of the process of exile, and nothing, absolutely nothing could stop them from following through their commitment to Islam.

It was all the better to test that commitment and to better demonstrate that they were destined to the sole Creator that this verse invoking the Muhajirat was revealed, in order to emphasise the absolute necessity of the criteria of 'sincerity' for this spiritual cause, with a strong political dimension. In fact, the Qur'an says on this subject:

> O YOU who have attained to faith! Whenever believing women come unto you, forsaking the domain of evil, examine them, [although only] God is fully aware of their faith; and if you have thus ascertained that they are believers, do not send them back to the deniers of the truth, [since] they are [no longer] lawful to their erstwhile husbands, and these are [no longer] lawful to them [...]. (al-Mumtaḥana 60: 10)

The classical exegeses report that this verse was revealed when two men from the Quraysh clan came to request the return of their sister, Umm Kulthum bint 'Aqaba, a convert to Islam who had emigrated towards Madinah in order to join the Muslim community.[23]

It is worth recalling that at this time the Prophet had made a pact of alliance, the pact of al-Hudaybiyyah, with the enemy

---

23. Al-Fassi, *Al-'Aqd al Matin*, in Ziyadah, *Dawr al-Mar'a as-Siyasi*, p. 151.

Quraysh tribe. Among the clauses of this pact, which advocated the cessation of war for ten years, it was stipulated that during this period any Qurayshis who joined the Prophet in Madinah without the permission of a legal guardian, should be extradited towards Makkah.

Umm Kulthum, who had converted on her own among all her family members and who had fled one of the most hostile environments, implored the Prophet not to return her to her people, in order not to have to relive the unjust treatment she had received.[24] The verse was thus revealed in order to stop the extradition of women who had converted to Islam in order not to expose them to the reprisals of their respective families, and the Prophet subsequently refused to return exiled women to the enemy clan, whereas the agreement was maintained for men.

Faced with the influx of women emigrating towards Medina, the Qurayshis began a veritable campaign of defamation against the women who went into exile and questioned the sincerity of their Hijrah, accusing them of debauchery and immorality.[25]

It was thus to cut short all of these disingenuous rumours, and to ensure that the commitment of these women to exile not be put into question, that God exhorted the Prophet to test the emigrating women in order to ascertain their sincerity, even if, as the Qur'an says, God is best Informed of their true motivation. According to the different *tafasīr*, the test in short consisted in making them attest that their exile was motivated purely by love for God and by faithfulness to His Prophet.

The Divine pedagogy sought to give a sense of responsibility to these women and remind them that their commitment to Islam was a commitment to endurance and resistance.

A pact to which they were in fact unanimously faithful, given the number of Muhajirat whom never ceased to flood from Makkah to Madinah despite extremely difficult geographical and climatic conditions, despite the dangerous mode of transport, the thirst, the hunger, the risk of attack and the unforeseen on the way.

---

24. *Tafsīr* of Tabari.
25. Ibid.

None of this stopped these women from cementing their aspirations and joining the nascent community of faith, in order to participate fully in the construction of the new, much anticipated society.

The historical testimony of the loyalty of these exiled women is poignant and is testament to this spiritual responsibility which was incumbent upon them since the historians unanimously affirm that none of the Muhajirat returned to the enemy clans of Makkah and that none of them was known to have betrayed the pact made with the Prophet on exile and its conditions.[26]

Exile as a political act was thus a means for the Muslim woman of the time to affirm her presence as an active member of society and ensure her complete contribution to the new concept of political action as it was instituted by Islam. She was not asked to *remain at home* in order to wait for men alone to erect the foundations of the new Muslim city!

Women were active participants in the story of exile, with all its adventures and their share of suffering and sacrifice, and this remains the indelible evidence of women's activism as it was promoted by the message of Islam. Islam which, contrary to what is said about it today, judges the abilities and intrinsic values of each and every one of us, outside of any consideration based on gender or race.

Political exile was certainly a historic *moment* engendered by the circumstances of the time and which ended with the victory of Muslims in this land of Hijaz, but the spirit of Hijrah is not obsolete and as the Prophet himself said in order to perpetuate this duty of exile in each and every one of us: *'The exiled is he who exiles himself from all the destructive and dangerous sides he has within him.'*[27]

In other words, one must know how to exile oneself in one's inner self while bearing in mind the state of mind which motivated these Muhajirat and Muhajirūn, knowing like them how to make sacrifices, renounce privileges, endure at times to be subjected to

---

26. According to imam az-Zuhri, see Ibn Ḥajjar, *Fath al-Bari*, chapter on the conditions during the treaties of peace, pp. 418–5.
27. Hadith reported by Ibn Māja and Nasa'i.

the worst, in order to *exile* oneself or *resist* all these numerous and insidious negative *forces* which make living our faith day to day often a real trial.

Only an *exile of the heart*, an *inner exile*, can alleviate, if not eradicate, this profound internal tension, the reflection of our resistance to a sometimes very aggressive outside world.

Knowing how to *exile oneself* sometimes, a self-exile from ourselves and others in order to ensure that our faith is less vulnerable, less fragile ... .

Perhaps this is what, among others, our *duty* of exile consists of today.

The *Mubayiʿat* or the political participation of women

The term *mubayiʿat* comes from *bayʿah*, also referred to as an 'act' or 'sermon of allegiance' and the *mubayiʿat* are the women who took the *bayʿah*. There were in fact many of them, all along the period of revelation, who came to pledge allegiance to the Prophet considered to be the leader of the Muslim community of the time.

The concept of *bayʿa*[28], from the Islamic perspective is essentially based around three dimensions: the representative of the community, the believers who make up the said community and the legislation around which the pact is made. Two principles underpin the validity of this pact: the principle of *shura* or 'consultation' between the head and the members of the community, and the principle of *ṭāʿa* or 'obedience' of the community to the leader. This principle of *ṭāʿa* is not absolute since it relies on the responsibility of the community which must be watchful that the leader respects the law. This is what is confirmed by the hadith of the Prophet where it is clearly stipulated *'there is no obedience to a human being in disobedience to the principles set by the Creator.'*

It is clear that over the course of Islamic history these principles were rarely respected to the letter and it is sad to say that the principle of *shura* was often reduced, even sidelined, to the detriment of that

---

28. The sermon of allegiance, in its traditional form, is still in use in the United Kingdom, for example, but also in the framework of naturalization ceremonies in the United States of America.

of *ṭāʿa*, excessively instrumentalized according to the discretion of the Amir.

The Prophet, out of a concern to 'institutionalize' solid and permanent links with the believers and granting legitimacy to the nascent Islamic alliance, established pacts with all those who, while accepting the message of Islam, had committed to respecting its rules, obligations and responsibilities. The contract of allegiance, as it was established by the Prophet, gave the believer a sense of responsibility since it was a voluntary and free act which allowed him subsequently to integrate a community of faith where all were equal and where all owed each other mutual assistance.

Islamic history references several commemorations of acts of *bayʿah* between the Prophet and the believers, male or female, from different regions and tribes, and this at different periods during the time of revelation.

On the subject of women *(mubayiʿat)*, the Qur'an provides certain directives concerning them in the following verse:

> *O Prophet! Whenever believing women come unto thee to pledge their allegiance to thee, [pledging] that [henceforth] they would not ascribe divinity, in any way, to aught but God, and would not steal, and would not commit adultery, and would not kill their children, and would not indulge in slander, falsely devising it out of nothingness: and would not disobey thee in anything [that thou declarest to be] right – then accept their pledge of allegiance, and pray to God to forgive them their [past] sins: for, behold, God is much-forgiving, a dispenser of grace. (al-Mumtahanah* 60: 12)

This verse is often cited as *the* reference concerning the *bayʿah* of women, sometimes called *bayʿaht an-nisa* and Imam Nawawi[29] considers this allegiance as being the most important legally speaking *(al-bayʿah ash-sharʾiyya)* since it contains directives at all levels, spiritually, socially and legally, capable of establishing the basis for a new conception of society.

---

29. *Sahih Muslim,* according to the commentary by an-Nawawi, p. 531.

It is worth noting here that this *bay'at an-nisa* was not the only one concerning women, and this despite the majority of works of Islamic history remaining very vague as to the actual number of acts of allegiance to which women participated.

In fact, all along the period of revelation there were several acts of allegiance during which women were actively involved. It seems, according to a recent study, that there have been at least five major events of this sort which we can consider as historical reference points, knowing all the while that the list cannot be exhaustive as it does not take into account all the times when the Prophet took the pledge of allegiance from women who had recently converted to Islam, in particular circumstances.[30]

There was first, during the early years of the revelation and before the first Hijrah, an initial *bay'ah* in Makkah, in the presence of fourteen women. As it was the beginning of the Prophetic mission, the pact essentially concerned the testimony of faith and faithfulness to the spiritual principles with all that flows from this in terms of a moral and ethical life.[31]

Then there was the *bay'at al-Aqaba*, which unfolded in several stages, and it is during the second that two women appear: Nusayba bint Ka'b, nicknamed Umm 'Umarah, and Asma bint 'Amr, among the seventy three men who came to pledge allegiance.[32] The conditions under which this *bay'at al-Aqaba* unfolded were among the most difficult, since the mission of the Prophet was still clandestine and the relentlessness of the Quraysh clan was at its apogee. This bellicose context of the time is why the Prophet imposed more arduous and demanding clauses during this pact. In fact, the Prophet asked the Muslims who were present to fight alongside him in the armed struggle against the enemy, to ensure his protection and assistance and to swear him loyalty whatever the sacrifices and hardships which might be incurred.

30. Ziyadah, *Dawr al-Mar'a as-Siyasi.*
31. The names of all of the *mubayi'at* – all pledges of allegiance included – are reported in the work of Ziyadah in the shape of a list of 388 women, itemized as the author indicates, from the classical work, *Al-Isaba* by Ibn Hajjar.
32. Ibid., p. 164.

Umm 'Umarah, present during this *bay'ah*, remained faithful all of her life to her commitment towards the Prophet and to Islam. During the battle of Uhud she was wounded thirteen times and the Prophet, seeing her struggle and fight despite all her injuries, said to her: '*Who else could endure all that you are suffering here Umm 'Umarah?*' During the same battle, she said of her: '*The rank of Umm 'Umarah is today higher than that of such and such!*'

She was present during all of the major events of the time, like al-Hudaybiyyah, Hunayn and during the battle of al-Yamama, during which she lost a hand.[33] Umm 'Umarah, a woman who fought on every front, was present everywhere: at the mosque, during the meetings called by the Prophet, on the battlefield ... She was always there where duty called her. This is the perfect example of a political participation which remains faithful to the pact signed with the Prophet of Islam, a faithfulness without fault, a faithfulness which fulfils its commitments.

After the exile to Madinah, the Prophet received delegations of women on several occasions, who came ready to pledge allegiance. The most famous *bay'ah* was that which coincided with the celebration of Eid and where the number of women present who participated in the pact must have been very significant since there was a representative for the women, speaking in their name and who was discussing the clauses of the pact with the Prophet.[34]

In Madinah, where it was a case of establishing the foundations for a new community unified by faith and respect for the values of justice and loyalty, the Prophet insisted on this occasion on the responsibility of each of these women towards the community. He encouraged the participants to reinforce their actions through acts of goodwill and financial support to the various nascent projects of this first city of Islam.

Then there was the *bay'at ar-ridwan*, the pact seeking God's approval, known under the name of *bay'at ash-shajarah* or the 'pact of the tree'.

---

33. Hadith in *at-Tabaqat*, p. 444; Muḥammad Sa'id Mabid, *Mawsu'at Hayat.*
34. According to the author of the study, it was Umm Salama al-Ansariyya as reported by Ibn Ḥajjar in a hadith by Tabarani.

This pact occurred during the conflict of al-Hudaybiyyah[35] and the main conditions were resistance to the enemy through the struggle or jihad, patience and endurance ... .

This *bay'ah* has a particular connotation since it is evoked in the Qur'an in very rewarding terms:

> *Behold, all who pledge their allegiance to thee pledge their allegiance to God: the hand of God is over their hands.*
> (*al-Fath* 48: 10)

Among the women who were present at this event, apparently numerous but with no exact figures available only the name of eight of them were recorded in the works of Islamic history.[36]

Finally, during the triumphant entry into Makkah, history records one of the greatest ceremonies of allegiance to which both men and women participated, initially in a solemn act of testimony of faith and faithfulness to the path of Islam.[37] And later, the Prophet respectively received the men and then the women.

It is thus worth noting that women participated very actively in the majority of allegiance ceremonies, even when it was a pact stipulating armed struggle, endurance and physical or material assistance to the Prophet and to his noble cause. There were no differences to the Prophet between the allegiance of a woman and that of a man, and he considered women as active and inescapable members of a community which was required to construct itself upon the foundations of this social equality.

But it is worth noting that when one studies the works of Islamic history, both ancient and recent, that the vast majority of authors struggle to conceive of an equal participation of women in this political process. They minimize this contribution, sometimes

---

35. Whereas the Prophet, accompanied by 1,500 believers, was camping at al-Hudaybiyyah 20 km outside of Makkah where he had decided to head in order to undertake the smaller pilgrimage of *'umrah*, the Quraysh refused them access to the Holy sites. Negotiations between the two parties ended with the signature of the treaty of al-Hudaybiyyah.
36. See *Dawr 'al-Mar'a as-Siyasi*, Ziyadah p. 180.
37. Same references, reported by Imam Ahmad, p. 182.

even ignore it and insist on very secondary considerations. This is the case notably of the interpretation of the verse cited above of the *bay'ah of women*, where the importance of the act in itself, notably 'the participation of women' in a political act of this type, is *diluted* in simplistic interpretations relative to the conditions of the allegiance.

In fact, if we closely examine the Qur'anic verse in question, one notes first the 'respectful approach' of the free choice of women. The verse begins with *'Oh Prophet! If believing women come to you to pledge allegiance to you.'* The 'if' reflects the conditionality of the act. If they come of their own will, then the pact will be valid. The women had come themselves to participate in this initiative, they were in no way forced to do so, even less so to follow their husbands, fathers or other male relatives.

A number of stories show how women converted without the knowledge of their husbands, even of their tribe, and how they experienced their commitment to Islam like a true rebellion against their own family.

In fact, the Prophet received these *mubayi'at* separately from the men in order to specifically honour this political *independence*. Given the social environment of the time, which considered that women should *follow* their fathers, husbands or other appointed *guardian*, the Prophet could have contented himself of an allegiance aimed at the men who would have been the legal *representatives* of these women. But he could not have acted in this fashion because he was always convinced of the necessity of the actual contribution of women. The verse revealed, thus, came to support him in his emancipating project for women. In receiving them separately, the Prophet was merely respecting the Divine pedagogy which was seeking to establish a new vision of women: that of a free, independent and responsible being.

This was a doubly telling act on the part of the Prophet who, in receiving them personally, sought to *cement* female political participation while showing that their *freedom of choice*, as women, was equally primordial.

The Qur'an mentions, still in the same verse, the conditions inherent to the pact, starting with one of the basic principles of any spiritual commitment, namely that of faith in One God. Then come the more general conditions by way of ethical principles, such as the forbidding of theft, of extra-conjugal sexual relations, of dishonesty, infanticide – notably of young girls, a widespread custom of the time – in other words, of all those acts universally recognized as being vile and condemnable.

Then the verse ends with a condition which constitutes in some ways a sort of Islamic mantra and which stipulates the acceptance by these *mubayi'at* of the decisions of the Prophet in all which can be considered as being part of the 'good', or the 'acceptable': *'And to not disobey you in the good (ma'rūf).'*

The term *ma'rūf* refers to a global concept, in other words what we frequently refer to as the *common good* which represents the basis of all ethical values and which encompasses all that which remains in conformity with an ideal of morals and justice. In this verse, God incites the participating women to obey the Prophet every time he enjoins them to invest in that good, the only guarantee of the general interest. It is interesting to see how God renders that *obedience conditional solely on the doing of good*, even when it comes to the Prophet known for his irreproachable moral integrity and who would never – ever – have encouraged immoral practises. This should make us think about those who advocate an *unconditional (tā'a) obedience* of the wife to the husband and who present this as a critical and inescapable principle for any pious Muslim woman, *as she should be*! A strange way to conceive of things when God has never advocated in His Holy book any sort of obedience – particularly not *absolute* obedience – of the wife towards the husband ... This authoritarian conception of a supposedly always *perfect* spouse to whom the wife, no matter the circumstance, owes obedience is rooted in a patriarchal culture which, from the beginning of time, has kept women in a state of permanent subordination and which seeks out through prefabricated religious concepts an infallible justification for its discriminatory practices.

And yet nowhere, in the Qur'an do we find, concerning conjugal relations, this conception of the subordination and enslavement of women to a husband supposedly beholden to all rights. Too often we forget that the Qur'an speaks of marriage as a 'heavy contract' *mithaq ghaliz*.[38] In this *mithaqun ghaliz*, there is firstly the notion of a pact and whomsoever speaks of a pact, suggests a partnership of equal parts. There is also this description of the pact as 'heavy', as if to better highlight the importance of the mutual commitment of both partners. It is interesting to note here the reach of this concept of *mithaqun ghaliz* which is used in the Qur'an in another verse concerning the commitment of the messengers towards their Creator.[39] The pact consecrated during marital life is just as significant as that which linked the messengers to the Creator!

The two partners, according to the Qur'anic vision, owe each other love and respect and must manage this contract through a mutual understanding capable of achieving the essential conditions for a serene and happy co-existence. In describing the relationship between the two spouses, God uses the term *taradi*, which means 'common agreement' several times in His holy Book, as well as the term *tashawur* or consultation.[40] The two spouses, after mutual consultation, agree on all the decisions which need to be taken, whatever their importance or gravity. The Qur'an, in this regard, provides us with a telling example with the question of the weaning of the baby which must be achieved after a common agreement of the two spouses.

There are the two principles *tashawur* and *taradi*, 'consultation' and 'common agreement' which, as the Qur'an stipulates, represents the foundation of all healthy and harmonious conjugal relationships and not a given blind obedience of the wife to her husband who sometimes becomes the symbol of a range of tyrannies and all the family related frustrations. If there is any obedience, it is that of the two partners towards He who created them and made them equal human beings.

To pretend that the husband, as a man, is superior to the woman through Divine preference and that the woman owes him

---

38. *Al-Nisā'* 4: 21.
39. *Al-Aḥzāb* 33: 7.
40. *Al-Nisā'* 4: 24; 2: 232–233.

obedience whatever the circumstances, is to lay claim to an obvious form of *idolatry*. Something which is clearly in total contradiction with the essence of the Qur'anic message, namely 'the unicity of God', or *tawḥīd*.

The alleged Divine preference afforded to men, affirmed on the basis of the well-known concept of 'precedence' or *qiwama*[41] of men over women, is in fact an *obligation*, of the order of *taklīf* in light of a financial obligation vis-à-vis the maintenance of the family home and not a particular honour (*tashrif*) afforded to men.

This term *qiwama* has often been translated erroneously as 'superiority' and the patriarchal reading has even elevated it to a state of *despotism* and rendered it a *sacred privilege* of the Muslim man.[E]

This is an important question which unfortunately has been dangerously instrumentalized by some Muslims. In fact, by *sacralizing* this concept of obedience of women known under the term *ṭāʿa*, the tenants of this type of discourse make this a religion of discrimination and make Muslim women feel guilty whereby, concerned with respecting their convictions, they experience the most humiliating kinds of injustices. Some scholars, certainly influenced by a misogynistic socio-cultural context, go so far as to compare the institution of marriage to a prison where man is the absolute *master* and the woman entirely subordinate to his power like a prisoner![42]

What is more, Islamic jurisprudence has gone very far in its restrictive vision of the conjugal union, elaborating one of the most abusive legal concepts, namely that of *bayt at-ṭāʿa* which can literally be translated as 'the residence of obedience', a veritable marital prison where the wife who requests a divorce and refuses to live with her husband can be forced to return to her husband's home by the police and by order of a court![43]

Although the forced return to the family home has today

---

41. *Al-Nisāʾ* 4: 34.
42. Ibn al-Qayyim al-Jawziyya, *Aʿlam al-Muwaqqiʾin*, II, p. 107.
43. A legal concept which was in place until recently in many personal status codes in Muslim countries, notably in Egypt.

disappeared, the concept of *ṭāʿa* or obedience, has remained one of the principal elements of the personal status code in a majority of Muslim countries.[44] In some personal status codes in practise in Muslim countries, if the wife *disobeys* her husband, the latter can cut off her sustenance![45]

We are far removed from the Qur'anic vision, which condemns all forms of despotism and injustice, and the bulk of the spiritual message of which urges justice and equity. This type of premise which advocates the imprisonment of women and their submission to unjust laws stems from a patriarchal despotism entirely comparable with that which emanates from authoritarian political powers.

What is more it is interesting at this level to draw the analogy between these two aspects of *ṭāʿa* that of the wife to the husband and that of the Muslim, male or female, to the political leader! In the Islamic jargon, the term *ṭāʿa* remains principally and narrowly linked to these two powers, that of the husband and that of the political leader.

These are two sides of the same coin and a certain Islamic *fiqh* entirely subject to the good will of the Amir will ensure that everything in Islam revolves around this concept of 'obedience' or *ṭāʿa*. What is more a woman who accepts and experiences humiliation is a woman who will transmit that same humiliation to future generations. A woman who accepts and experiences injustice within the home is a woman who will educate her children to accept all these injustices. She will render them beings predisposed to accepting all forms of submission and dictatorships.

Concerning the principle of *non-disobedience* towards 'good' (*marʿūf*); as it was prescribed at the end of the verse, it is often interpreted in a very reductive manner in numerous texts of Qur'anic commentary. In fact, it is interesting to note how some exegetes have *reduced* the significance of this principle to solely the forbidding of the practise of *wailing*, common to certain funeral rituals among the Arabs of the time.

---

44. See the Algerian, Jordanian, Egyptian, Kuwaiti, Syrian, etc. codes.
45. See the Egyptian personal status code.

This custom was known under the name of *niyaha* and we find in virtually all the classical works the interpretation by Ibn ʿAbbas who reports concerning the *'principle of the non-disobedience to marʿūf'* that the women had made a commitment to the Prophet to no longer undertake this custom of wailing or *niyaha*.[46]

It is true that there exists in the tradition of the Prophet a narration by a woman named Umm ʿAtiyya al-Ansariya who evokes, among the clauses of the pact to which she was a witness, the prohibition of this practise of *niyaha*.

It also remains true that during the pre-Islamic period, the Arab women would traditionally accompany the body of the deceased person with cries, tears and moans of supplication, going so far as to tear their clothes or lacerating their face. Some among them were paid to do this and others did this as a *favour* to a friend who needed assistance in *mourning their dead*.[47]

Umm ʿAtiyya was known among the women of her tribe for this sort of practise, hence the assertion by the Prophet with her regard.[48] By insisting on the prohibition of this custom, the Prophet was merely educating Muslim women to have greater restraint and rigour in their behaviour. Through his sense of pedagogy, he sought to transform the ancestral tribal customs through spiritual elevation and moral decency. Forbidding this sort of custom was to learn to suffer in silence, it was to cry while retaining dignity. It was also a way of ensuring *acceptance* of the idea of death, accepting Divine will, while preserving hope of a reunion in a next world certainly better for those who know how to be patient.

A classical commentator by the name of al-Qurṭubi, criticized in his exegesis the simplistic reduction of the concept of *marʿūf* and clarified that the Prophet was merely adapting his discourse to each group of people. In this regard and to illustrate his point, he

---

46. See *tafsīr* of Tabari and Ibn Kathir, the narration of Ibn ʿAbbās concerning the term *marʿūf*.
47. It is interesting to remember that this custom is universal and reports of it date back to antiquity where the wailers were women who would implore the sky by groaning and crying during the funeral. In some rural regions of the Arab world, this tradition still persists despite its prohibition in Islam.
48. Ibn Kathir, *Tafsīr*, commentary of the verse in question.

gave the example of the pact undertaken with the men belonging to the tribe of 'Abd al-Qays, known for their excessive dependence on alcoholic drinks, and for which the Prophet included in the pact the prohibition of the consumption of alcohol and demanded that this condition be made a priority.[49]

It is obvious that it is not a case here of putting into question the veracity of this interpretation given by one of the first and most illustrious exegetical scholars as was Ibn 'Abbas. The latter was in fact one of the founders of the school of exegesis based on the tradition of the Prophet – ahl al-hadith – or the 'people of hadith'. He thus scrupulously interpreted the verse according to the tradition of the Prophet (narration by Umm 'Atiyya). But the risk which this type of strictly *traditionalist* interpretation of observance can sometimes encounter is to drastically reduce the significance of the verse, knowing all the while that some hadiths, such as this one, remains limited to particular circumstances. Al-Qurtubi who, while belonging to this school of ahl al-hadith, leaves room for personal judgement in his exegesis, hence his refusal to accept this narrow conception of mar'uf.

What is more, it is worth clarifying that the content of the verse on bay'ah concerning women was used by the Prophet on several occasions, and this as much for women as for men. The tradition reports that during the first pact of 'Aqaba, to which only men were present, the latter accepted the sermon according to the same criteria outlined in the said verse.[50]

The content is, therefore, not *specific* to women and despite the historical vagueness which prevails concerning bay'ah an-nisa, relating to the diversity of contexts and the true participation of women, it remains that the message of the verse is clear: the

---

49. Exegesis of al-Qurtubi, concerning the verse in question. Other scholars are of the same opinion as this scholar, like Dahhak, narration reported by Tabari and Wahb ibn Jarir in Ibn Kathir.

50..*Tafsīr*, Ibn Kathir, p. 327. Narration reported by Ahmad and confirmed in *Sahih Bukhari* and *Sahih Muslim*. Ibn Kathir confirms according to a narration by 'Ubada ibn as-Samit, that the conditions of the bay'ah were the same during the first 'Aqaba as those of bay'at an-nisa, as prescribed in surah al-Mumtahana.

political participation of Muslim women is required in the same way as that of men. It is in itself an act of faith and a duty for all Muslim women who feel that the message of Islam is relevant to them.

From its outset Islam has integrated women into the *election* procedure of the head of the Muslim community, since the *bay'ah*, according to the vision of Islam, is a legal process in which the Muslim leader promises to respect the laws and the will of the people in exchange for the allegiance allotted to him. But what happened after the death of the Prophet? Where are the other *bay'at* in which Muslim women participated? They simply did not occur. It is unfortunate to note that the political participation of women, advocated by the Qur'an and so dear to the Prophet, remained at the stage of a *project* which was rapidly buried shortly after the death of the Prophet!

One cannot help but ask oneself what really happened during the history of Islam for such central principles, as those which advocate the political participation of women, to have become marginalized in this way and sometimes become perceived as even *anti-Islamic*. Despite the presence of major directions within the guiding Qur'anic principles for a veritable social, as well as political emancipation of women, these very same principles have since become synonymous with oppression and eternal discrimination!

The terrifying regression observed throughout history concerning the status of women, as well as the current situation in many Muslim countries – particularly those said to be strict as concerns Islamic legislation and where the political participation of women remains forbidden – are indicative of the decline of Islamic thought and the inability of Muslims to elaborate a coherent and fair vision of their religion.[51]

According to classical exegeses and still concerning this verse of the *bay'ah*, we note the presence of certain hadiths which inform us of the particular modalities relative to the allegiance of women.

---

51. This is the case of Kuwait which has just recently afforded women the right to vote after years of debate and a relentless opposition to the project coming predominantly from the Islamist parliamentary group.

Indeed, for men the *bay'ah* was traditionally concluded by a handshake between the assigned representatives and the members of the community who chose them, a sign that the pact had been accepted by the parties concerned.

As for the women, no pact was concluded through the traditional handshake required to indicate the conclusion of the agreement, and this for reasons personal to the Prophet who, after each sermon of allegiance with women, informed them orally of its acceptance. The most famous hadith on this topic is that which, in several reference works, cites the version of 'Ā'ishah, wife of the Prophet, according to which she clarifies that the Prophet never extended his *hand* for the women's *bay'ah* and that he formulated his approval verbally.[52]

Beyond the symbolic dimension of the Prophet's attitude which surely represents a moral norm, it is interesting to note how this act took on disproportionate proportions in Islamic studies, particularly the more recent variety, to the extent of marginalising, even entirely discrediting the political act of *bay'ah*!

Writings on women's *bay'ah* are focused primarily on the question of the *handshake*, known under the name *musafaha*, which led to a prolific literature erected around what has become a veritable moral slogan, namely the prohibition of handshaking between individuals of the opposite sex. The central and primary idea in any historical study of the *bay'ah* of women in Islam resides in this event henceforth deemed crucial, and this *lack of a handshake for women* has completely masked what was a revolution for the mores of the time, namely the political participation of women. This participation subsequently became secondary, sometimes even insignificant, in the eyes of many contemporary scholars.

Some have even tried to justify the *invalidity* of the *bay'ah* by sole virtue of the fact that the Prophet did not shake hands with the women![F] This absence of a handshake signifies, according to them, that the pact of allegiance with the women was a mere formality and that its content could be summarized by a simple religious moral code of the order of social conventions. Others have extracted this

52. *Sahih Bukhari*, Book of Divorce, chapter *Bay'at an-Nisa*.

action by the Prophet from the entire major story of the *bay'ah* in order to make of it the moral and unconditional basis of true piety and the currency of a good Muslim, practising, demanding and concerned with respecting the minor detail of the principles of Islam and behaviour of the Prophet.

The assertion according to which women's *bay'ah* is minimized by the absence of a handshake is an assertion which is false in itself, since the historic testimony is undeniable. Any analysis of the political events of the time indicates that women's act of allegiance was a symbolically powerful moment in the history of Islam, and that the absence of a handshake cannot be a justification for annulling the validity of this act, recognized by the Qur'an, the Prophet and the historic testimonials by the earliest Muslim scholars.

Such an assertion which excludes the entire logic of the insertion of women into political work and their active participation in the development of their society, and which priorities very secondary considerations, is sadly symptomatic of the intellectual poverty currently raging in so-called Islamic societies. Whereas the Prophet was diligent in applying Qur'anic principles and worked tirelessly to ensure the social and political participation of women in the project of a just and ethical society, the only thing retained is the absence of a hand shake between him and the women!

It is not a case of wishing to underestimate or demeaning an interpersonal *problem* faced by many Muslims, male and female, sincere and committed to imitating the model of the Prophet, but it is about criticising those who make of it a priority and a formal obligation to the detriment of far more important principles for Islam and Muslims.

To sacrifice all this historic potential which, 1,500 years ago, raised the status of women and encouraged her to stand alongside men in any foundational project concerning the new community is, in addition to being unjust towards Muslims themselves, truly damaging in the eyes of the rest of humanity who see in Islam a codified religion, mummified and fossilized.

A religion which sacrifices the majority of its time, of its energy and its skills in debating superficialities when the real substantive debates, those likely to engender progress, are cruelly lacking ... .

To reduce the essence of the message of Islam, like that of this encouragement of women's participation in politics, to a prohibition on greeting members of the opposite sex with a handshake, is really to do a disservice to Islam by providing all those who make this their *Trojan horse*, an opportunity to denigrate the faith.

Al-Mujadilah, when God listens to the secrets of a woman

The tradition relates the story of Khawlah bint Tha'laba who one day came to see the Prophet to complain about her husband.[53] According to the narration related by 'Ā'ishah, mother of the believers, Khawlah came to confide at length in the Prophet, telling him how her husband, after many years together, had one evening offended her by comparing her to 'the back of his mother'. This expression, known as *zihar*, was widely used by the pagan Arabs who, in order to divorce, compared their wives to 'the back of their mothers'.

This custom automatically rendered the woman forbidden for life to her husband, and yet did not allow her to dispose of herself freely, nor even to remarry. In a long confession to the Prophet, Khawlah expressed her deep sadness at seeing how, after all these years of common union with her husband, having offered him her best years, he had rejected her when she was no longer youthful.[54]

After hearing this confession by a woman wounded in her pride, the Prophet received the revelation of Surah *al-Mujadilah*. A Divine revelation which came to answer the fears of this woman and to prove once again that God is here, always, so Close, so Present, attentive to all ... .

---

53. The narration is found in virtually all the works of commentaries according to versions which differ only slightly but which remain broadly the same. The version related here is that narrated by 'Ā'ishah. See Tabari, *Tafsīr*, concerning the circumstances of the revelation of Sura *al-Mujadilah*.

54. See the text in Arabic of Khawlah's lament, according to the version reported by 'Ā'ishah, reported by among others Ibn Kathir, in his *Tafsīr* of Surah *al-Mujadilah*.

The verse in question responds to Khawlah's quest in the following terms:

> GOD *has indeed heard the words of her who pleads with thee concerning her husband, and complains Unto God. And God does hear what you both have to say: verily, God is all-hearing, all-seeing. As for those of you who [henceforth] separate themselves from their wives by saying, "Thou art as unlawful to me as my mother', [let them bear in mind that] they can never be [as] their mothers: none are their mothers save those who gave them birth: and so, behold, they but utter a saying that runs counter to reason, and is [therefore] false [...].*
> (al-Mujadilah 58: 1-2)

These verses highlight several important principles. Firstly, that of the listening and respect of this woman's grievance, that of her right to freedom of expression and then that of the immediate social reform, commanded by God, of the removal of this humiliating custom for women.

As regards this last point the Qur'an immediately condemned what is, henceforth, considered as a grave error, while indicating the different modalities of its expiation in the subsequent verses of the same surah.[55]

God thus responds to the expectation of this woman by firmly criticising this sort of customary expression which He refers to as 'blame-worthy' and 'false', all the while prescribing strict sanctions in order to discourage those who struggled to rid themselves of it.

The Creator, from the height of His Heavens, has therefore listened and attributed importance to the concerns of this woman who had come to confide her intimate problems to the Prophet. The latter was just as obliging and attentive to her suffering but also to that of others, of all the others, especially that of the women towards whom he devoted a special indulgence and an avowed tenderness.

---

55. This expiation is, according to the abilities of each person: the freeing of a slave, the observance of fasting for two months consecutively, or to feed sixty poor people.

God and His Prophet were *attentive* to believers and revelation shows us here the necessity, even the obligation, of listening to others whatever their discourse may be, their query or the depth of intimacy of their suffering.

How many women with broken hearts, bruised by daily humiliations of this same type, stay quiet and lock themselves in profound silence, simply because they have not found a sympathetic ear? Because, in the name of Islam, it is often *poorly viewed*, especially for a woman, to expose and reveal her problems, her expectations, her intimate issues and her internal conflicts. This *intimate confessions* side of Islam with all its compassion and tenderness is often as not always marginalized, if not entirely omitted, to the detriment of cold rigor which has ended up becoming the dominant image of the core of the Islamic message. Words like love, compassion, tenderness and intimacy are often absent in Islamic terminology, whereas verses like this one testify to a Divine proximity touching through its intimacy, thoughtfulness and benevolence.

The other principle highlighted by this verse is women's right to freedom of expression. This is a very revealing aspect of the state of mind of Islam's spiritual message which explains the latitude afforded to Muslim women at this time to freely manifest their ideas, their demands and their disquietudes.

In fact, Khawlah could have confided her pain to other women, some of whom surely would have experienced the same marital disillusionment, or else transmitted her missive to one of the wives of the Prophet, who would have approached him about it. But this was not the case precisely because the strength of faith and the growing hope in the new message allowed Khawlah to overcome the constraints naturally linked to the intimate realm. Khawlah had the courage to seek refuge by the Prophet and from there, to make her words heard by God Himself. By complaining to the Prophet about an ancestral custom, she was denouncing in her name, but also in the name of all the others, an unfair and oppressive practise which was known at the time as a specific form of repudiation and which, far from being a conjunctural custom, persists until this day under other just as deplorable manifestations.

This female testimony of the time reveals the degree of intellectual maturity of these believing women who, inspired by the light of their faith, had the moral courage to protest, denounce and contest an established order through unjust patriarchal customs.

This was the birth of a new feminine consciousness which rebelled in the name of faith and Islam's principle of justice. Surah *al-Mujadilah* is the footprint of this new feminine Islamic way of thinking which the Qur'an sought to instate progressively, but surely, along the twenty-three years of revelation.

The examples of Muslim women who, in the early years of revelation, used their freedom of expression and demonstrated incredible autonomy in terms of their choices as women, are numerous in the stories of the Prophetic tradition. But it is regrettable to see that these models of women pass almost unnoticed in classical Islamic literature. Mostly, they are only mentioned to illustrate other events and not with the specific objective of highlighting this veritable approach of feminine liberation. Some female figures who were central in Islamic history from the beginning of revelation though are mentioned continuously, not as references in their own right but as *secondary* figures, passive actors in history, even subaltern figures in comparison with the masculine representations considered to be the norm!

As an illustration of this *freedom of feminine expression*, we can cite two accounts reported in the classical works of hadith which provide very telling teachings on this subject.

Here is the story of Barira, a servant of Ā'ishah, the wife of the Prophet, and whom the latter had just freed. Barira was married to a young man by the name of Mugith whom she had never loved. By freeing her from her former servitude, the Prophet left her the choice between continuing life together with her spouse or divorce. She chose to separate from the one who'd been imposed on her against her will while she was a slave, but Mugith remained deeply in love with Barira and the tradition recounts that he would follow her everywhere, his beard full of never-ending tears. Moved by this scene, the Prophet asked his uncle al-'Abbas who was with him: 'Are you not surprised by Mugith's love for Barira and her hatred for him?' Al-'Abbas then suggested he try and reconcile them, which is what the Prophet sought to do. He asked Barira: *'Why not get back together with Mugith?'* – *'I am only here to intercede in your favour,'* he said to her. To which Barira responded: *'If that is so, then no, I do not want him.'*[56]

This is an example of a determined Muslim woman, making choices in the name of the freedom and rights given to her by Islam, an Islam which doubly freed her from submission to slavery and to that of the customs linked to forced marriage. She said **no** to the Prophet, all the while being careful to assess things clearly, distinguishing between what is of the order of the Prophetic mission and what is of the order of simple human mediation. Outside of an order which might have served the cause of Islam, she was unwilling to concede on her freedom to choose, including at the behest of the Prophet of Islam! The latter, respectful of precisely this right to freedom of choice as a fundamental right for all human beings and principally towards women who were the most vulnerable, did not use his power of dissuasion, as a Prophet, to influence her or intimidate her and force her to accept! This detail on his part: *'I am only here to intercede in your favour'* reveals the extent of the Prophet's respect for the rights of women to freedom of expression and is also testimony to the nobility of his soul.

Another example in the same vein is that of a hadith which relates the story of a young girl who came to see the Prophet to complain that her father had married her to her cousin without her consent. The Prophet gave her the choice of separating from her husband is such was her desire. She had this surprising response for him:

> "*I finally accepted this marriage but I wanted, by complaining, to show women that our fathers have no decisions to take in our place.*"[57]

---

56. This story is a hadith recounted in *Sahih Bukhari* in the chapter on divorces, p. 359.
57. Ibn Majah, *Sunan*.

This type of discourse, it is true, remains unbelievable when we know the reality of contemporary Muslim societies. Societies which, in the majority of cases, remain regulated by the most retrograde legal codes which run counter to the principles of freedom advocated in Islam. The examples in the current reality of a number of Muslim countries are more than telling, since it is in these countries that we find the most forced marriages, or arranged marriages for family reasons, which are still fashionable in many Islamic circles.

When one sees the damage engendered by the number of forced marriages still undertaken even in Muslim communities living in the West, one can be justifiably perplexed and stunned by the state of ignorance which reigns within them. What's more, it is impressive to see how these forced marriages, denounced by all international human rights associations, are actually representative of the oppression of Muslims by this religion, the source of all the woes which Islam has become. But how can we possibly be offended by these judgements, flawed as they may be, when it is Muslims themselves who, profoundly convinced of the *Islamic* nature of this practise, blithely propagate this sort of prejudice erroneously attributed to Islam?

In the spring of 2005, the grand Mufti of Saudi Arabia denounced the practise of forced marriage of women (according to which the male *legal guardian*, such as the brother or father imposes a choice of husband) which he judged to be *un-Islamic* and a source of great *injustice*. After this *fatwa*, Saudi Arabia banned forced marriages ... In 2005!

We have a right to ask ourselves why wait 1,500 years to prohibit the practise when the sacred surahs could not have been clearer on this topic?

The message of Islam's respect for a woman's unequivocal right to choose her future spouse and for her right to freedom of expression, contrasts with that which is propagated – and which continues to be today – by a certain Islamic culture which never ceases to demonstrate the exact opposite, namely that a Muslim woman has no right to either freedom of expression, or to choose her partner.

In many Muslim countries, women, whatever their social status, are legal minors as they remain under the tutelage of a man: husband, father or brother. The latter have the right – all the rights – to speak and choose in their name, to decide what will be better – and sometimes worse – for women. All of this is endorsed of course by a biased reading of religion which affords a guarantee of choice to the fervent defenders of women's subjugation.

Of course, when reforms occur in these countries in order to prohibit these sorts of practises, these are applauded and the state in question is praised for making important progress towards modernity, since it is *freeing itself from obscurantist religious laws*!

The recent reform of the family code in Morocco is an edifying example of this. This reform was the result of a consensus and a long process of consultation between different social, political and religious actors of the country under the aegis of the king. But, we must not forget that this process is, first and foremost, the fruit of a long struggle by secular feminist movements in this country, who denounce the retrograde status of Moroccan women in this code. These secular women did so in the name of their conscience, far from all religious references, whereas those who belonged to so-called Islamist or traditionalist political movements refused the change in the name of Islam and even denounced it, accusing it of being first and foremost western in nature! These practising women refused the reform because in their eyes it represented being placed under Western tutelage and they reacted out of fear for their religious identity! They defended the discrimination in the code because it was stipulated in the name of religion, despite the fact this same code was only one interpretation, among many others, of the Islamic sources, themselves restricted by the Maliki jurisprudential school. One can effectively denounce a certain hegemonic Western vision without simultaneously legitimising discriminatory practises which in addition are in contradiction with the core principles of Islam!

It is sad to see how Islam as a religion is relentlessly accused of wrongs of which it is undeniably innocent. Some Muslim intellectuals claim that all these discriminatory practises are in fact inherent to the sacred text whereas others seek to justify these same practises through theological alibis, all the while claiming explanations of the sort: Islam only seeks to *protect* women!

In fact, it is very common to find books describing Muslim women as a pearl, a gem in a jewellery box or a flower which requires protecting, defending, saving from an eternal external enemy. She can even be locked away, imprisoned; it is always for her own good, always to protect her. But the Qur'an has never spoken of women as flowers or jewels which need protecting!

The Qur'anic vision of women is in total opposition to this infantilising image propagated by a given Islamic culture. In Islam, women are first and foremost free human beings, gifted with sense, intelligence and reason. The example of Khawlah, this woman for whom surah *al-Mujadilah* was revealed, can in itself counter these aberrations. In denouncing an oppressive practise for women, she used her right to freedom of expression and Divine revelation anticipated a veritable social reform in her favour. What is more, Khawlah, a woman with a very strong personality and who surely emerged reinforced by this surah revealed *specifically for her*, felt confident enough to lecture someone like 'Umar ibn al-Khattab, years later, when he was himself leader of the believers!

What is reported in the traditional works of exegesis such as that of al-Qurtubi which refers to a veritable 'exhortation to good' was preached by the same Khawlah when she encountered the emir accompanied by a cortege of important men and publicly addressed him: 'Oh 'Umar, we called you 'Umayr (nickname of 'Umar) and then we called your 'Umar and today we refer to you using your title of Amir of the believers. So precisely because of this, you must always live in fear of God ... .'[58]

'Umar ibn al-Khattab, in fact, listened to her attentively and at length until she was finished, which led one of his companions who was surprised that someone like the Amir of the believers might waste their time listening to a strange old woman in the street! 'Umar responded to him in these terms:

---

58. *Tafsir* of Qurtubi, Surah *al-Mujadilah*.

"Woe to you! Do not you know that this woman is none other than Khawlah whose complaint was heeded by God from the height of His seven Heavens! How could I not listen to her when the Creator did?! I swear by God that if she retained me until nightfall, I would stay, only excusing myself to undertake the obligatory prayers!'[59]

The narrative of this meeting between 'Umar ibn al-Khattab and Khawlah, replete with its teachings, allows us to dispense with superfluous commentary. These two beings, equal before the Creator, had understood and assimilated the essence of the message of Islam. Would such a relationship, testimony to the spiritual, social and political equality as it was understood at the time, even be conceivable today, between a head of state and a citizen, between a Muslim man and a Muslim woman?

And the other verses?
What about the other verses, those which are immediately evoked as soon as one speaks of Islam and women? Those which are described as polemical and which are trotted out whenever one has the misfortune of trying to defend women's status in Islam?

Verses, vectors of the eternal accusation of an Islam which oppresses women and which finally and unfortunately have succeeded in overshadowing the entire remainder of the Qur'anic message. Of course, since in the Qur'an, polygamy is accepted, women inherit half of what men do, the testimony of a man is worth that of two women, a husband can beat his wife, *lightly* of course, but still strike her!

The statement is enlightening and the conclusions drawn from this superficial and smugly scathing perception are so persuasive, that it is often hard to *defend oneself*, let alone to debate them!

It is not my objective here to enter into the minor detail of each of these so-called problematic concepts. That would require a book in and of itself based on in-depth research, combined with critical

---

59. *Tafsīr* Ibn Kathir, Surah *al-Mujadilah*.

analysis, which would draw as much on classical commentaries as on the very prolific contemporary writings on this topic.[60]

What is more, an exhaustive study would be misplaced here when the objective of this book is first and foremost a modest attempt at *deconstruction* of certain *mythical concepts*, drawing on a new approach to the sacred text.

The subject of this essay is thus a re-reading in light of the entire message which, as we have seen, forged a new conception of feminine identity. Since the creation of the first human being, through the historical representations of very telling female figures through to the different initiatives created in order to forge a better perception of the *feminine*, the Qur'anic message has undoubtedly erected a new vision of women, based on greater justice and autonomy. A very *liberating* vision for the time – and even until today since the emancipation of women only really began at the turn of the twentieth century in the most advanced[61] countries – and the central intention was undeniably to progressively free women from a fundamentally unjust patriarchal system.

How then can we conceive that there might be verses which run counter to this requirement of justice, an inescapable pillar of Islam's spiritual message? The verses which refer to polygamy, to inheritance, to testimony and to the alleged rights of a husband to admonish his wife, are they in fact in contradiction with the rest? Are these verses truly unjust against women?

In fact, if we take these verses in isolation, if we extract them from the entirety of the text and if one undertakes a literalist reading which fails to take into account either the entirety of the Qur'anic message, or its driving principles, one might be tempted to answer yes. However, if one takes care to read and understand these verses in light of their respective contexts and in relation to their meaning and the higher objective of the holistic Qur'anic

---

60. One of recent most well researched and complete publications on this topic is that of Dr Shayma' al-Sarraf, *Ahkam al-Mar'a Bayna al-Ijtihad wa Taqlid*, in Arabic (comparative study in jurisprudence, *fiqh* and social sciences), (Paris: Editions Al-Qalam, 2001).

61. The Canon law of 1917 in force until 1983 considered women as struck by *imbecillitas*, a term in ancient law meaning 'congenital mental infirmity'.

message, the answer is certainly no.

In these types of verses in particular, one cannot avoid the work involved in a holistic reading. There are verses which require being studied in conjunction with other verses and in light of the Prophetic tradition. A single verse, isolated from the remainder of the text can lead to a relatively different interpretation, even a contradictory one from that undertaken from a range of verses and general information. In fact, a jurisprudential principle in Islam states that the verses of the Qur'an explain one another.

The literalist interpretation cannot transmit the core of the message because it ignores the core principles which constitute the internal structure of the text. God, in His Qur'an, has in fact outlined the modalities of this interpretation by underlining the necessity of a profound understanding of the message:

> *And upon thee [too] have We bestowed from on high this reminder, so that thou might make clear unto mankind all that has ever been thus bestowed upon them, and that they might take thought.* (al-Naḥl 16: 44)

We note in this verse three successive stages: that of revelation (the text), then that of the explanation by the Prophet (the interpretation) and finally that of reflection by people (the understanding).

This approach outlined by the Qur'an is the opposite of the literalist approach which stops at the mere meaning of the word. The literalist reading, which is a reading which stops at the *exteriority* of the term (*zahir*), is a reading which requires no questioning of the profound meaning which, for its part, represents the *interiority* (*batin*) of the word. Imam Abu Hamid al-Ghazali in his book *Mishkat al-Anwar* says that the literalist reading (*zahir*) without a spiritual, internal reading (*batin*) is a mutilation of the message!

The understanding of the Qur'an thus remains intimately linked to its internal coherence which remains in fact determined by a certain number of rules which must be respected if one wishes to discern and understand the true meaning of the message. One of these rules is the study of the texts – the Qur'an and Prophetic traditions – in their *entirety*, it is what the scholars have called *ash-shumuliyya*, that which allows an approach to the text according to a holistic vision.

In his methodology of *tafsīr*, Shaykh Yūsuf al-Qaradāwī refers, through degrees of importance, to the interpretation of the Qur'an by the Qur'an itself, then Qur'anic interpretation through the authentic tradition or *al-sunnah al-sahihah*, respect for the general meaning of the verse or *siyaq al-ayah*, and interest in the knowledge of circumstances of the revelation or *asbab an-nuzul*.[62]

Another approach to the Qur'an, which must be taken into account during the interpretation of a given verse, is that of the Qur'anic philosophy of change or the pedagogy of gradualism: *sunnat al-tadarruj*. This is a principle fundamentally grounded in the Qur'an and which translates the Divine will to undertake changes according to the law of progression. Aside from the immutable basic principles like Divine unicity, worship and universal ethical values, for all the remainder, the Qur'an appeals to the gradual changing of customs and usual practises in order to better prepare the human conscience to the required transformations.

Polygamy

To correctly interpret the verse of the Qur'an referring to polygamy, one must bear in mind the context of the time, which was *very favourable* to this custom, and its profound anchoring in the Bedouin Arab culture. The verse referring to polygamy, an ancestral pre-Islamic custom, which Islam did not introduce but, rather, that it sought to reduce the legitimacy of, is a typical example of the underlying philosophy of gradual change promoted by the Qur'an.

The Qur'an sought to respect the social order in place, which was very permissive with relation to marital and extra-marital relations, while erecting a new approach to the marital union conditioned by very strict principles. Limiting the number to four women in the framework of a respectful marriage and especially, to imperatively condition this permission on the absolutely equal

---

62. Dr Yūsuf al-Qaradawi, *Kayfa nata'amal ma'a al-Qur'an al-'Azim*, (Cairo: 2nd edition, Dar al-Shuruq, 2000, p. 215.

treatment between the wives: this was a first dissuasive stage which allowed the avoidance of brutal social ruptures and in particular the refusal to bend to it. What emerges from this verse is a certain inclination towards prohibition:

> [...] if you have reason to fear that you might not be able to treat them with equal fairness, then [only] one [...].
> (al-Nisā' 4: 3)

These restrictive modalities sought in principle to discourage all those who perceived, in the depths of their soul and conscience, the central intention of this verse, namely the strict respect for fairness and justice. This verse clearly stipulates that monogamy is the exemplary manifestation of a just marriage.

What's more, the context of the revelation of this verse, after the war of Uhud, is intimately linked to the oppression of orphan women whom the Qur'an sought first and foremost to protect from any abusive relationships. A temporary solution for a given context where the protection of orphans and widows was primordial. This exceptional permission had to be abrogated by conjunctural changes since the primary objective of this verse was to preserve justice and it is undeniable that marrying several women, outside of the specific circumstances of the time, was to take the risk of falling into injustice and of infringing the Divine prescriptions which are intransigent towards injustice. Another verse in fact confirms this human incapacity towards absolute equity between spouses:

> And it will not be within your power to treat your wives with equal fairness, however much you may desire it [...].
> (al-Nisā' 4: 29)

It is clear that through the wording of this verse, the Qur'an stipulates that polygamy leads to injustice and this, regardless of the husband's degree of probity. This is one of the examples of the Divine pedagogy which seeks to establish its objectives gradually but all the while making compromises and dealing with human reality. Read in this fashion, one understands that the Qur'an sought to relegate this custom which, in itself, can only be a source of injustices, by promoting monogamous unions as the ideal to aspire to for all Muslims faithful to Islamic ethics and concerned with respecting Divine injunctions.

Polygamy, taken in this context, was thus a concession to the general rule which is to limit oneself to one wife. In fact, did the Prophet not express his strong disapproval of polygamy when he learnt that 'Ali, husband to his daughter Fatima Zahra, wished to marry a second wife?

Despite the dissuasive Qur'anic measures towards polygamy, it is unfortunate to see throughout Islamic history and until today, the inappropriate undertaking of this practise and the innumerable prejudices caused as much within Muslim societies, as at the level of the image of Islam as a spiritual message. Polygamy has single-handedly and on a global scale become synonymous with Islam and the inevitable means through which to discredit the religion. Some Muslims themselves have very little or no understanding of the Qur'anic instructions in favour of a gradual disappearance of this practise and marrying more than one woman has become for some, a virtual favour decreed by God. The verse on polygamy is a prototype of the so-called conjuncture verses which cannot be extrapolated to our current reality as is the case for other verses of this sort such as slavery, war spoils, corporal punishment,[63][G] etc.

Some Muslim scholars have even considered the need to suspend or even abrogate this practise in our current context due to its poor interpretation by some Muslims, the negative consequence on the family and social front and finally also because it ends up representing a veritable psychological obstacle to the spread and understanding of the message of Islam.[64]

---

63. On this subject see the proposal by Tariq Ramadan in his call for a moratorium on corporal punishment and the death penalty in the Muslim world: www.tariqramadan.com.

64. Imam Muḥammad 'Abduh and other scholars, like the reformist and nationalist Allal al-Fasi in his book, *Self Critique* (*An-Naqd al-dhati,*) (Morocco: Editions al-Risalah, 1979).

Testimony

To claim that in Islam, the testimony of two women is equivalent to that of a single man on the basis of a single and unique verse is, in addition to being extremely reductive, totally erroneous. In fact, the verse in question says the following:

> *O YOU who have attained to faith! Whenever you give or take credit for a stated term, set it down in writing. [...] And call upon two of your men to act as witnesses; and if two men are not available, then a man and two women from among such as are acceptable to you as witnesses, so that if one of them should make a mistake, the other could remind her.* (al-Baqarah 2: 282)

Firstly, it is worth noting that the verse in question doesn't refer to testimony (*shahādah*) strictly speaking but rather to attestation (*ish-had*). There is a difference between the two acts.

Testimony is an action which occurs before a judge who, alone, is authorized to decide the veracity or the validity of the said testimony. In Islam, testimony, according to this legal procedure, is recognized outside of all considerations of this nature. What is taken into account by the judge is the intrinsic value of the witness and the validity of his deposition, whether the witness is male or female.

The verse in question refers to an act completely distinct from testimony, namely attestation established between two peoples in the case of a financial debt.

The majority of scholars concur on the fact that this verse refers to instructive (irshad[65]) considerations and has no legislative remit. It is addressed on the basis of instructions or advice aimed at creditors. [H]

In fact, financial transactions of this type relate to the private economic domain and the verse encourages the creditor to protect himself through an attestation, in good and due form, in order

---

65. For greater detail, see the work of the Egyptian intellectual Muḥammad 'Umarah, *at-Taḥrir al-Islami lil Mar'a*, (Cairo: Dar ash-Shurūq 2002, p. 82).

to preserve his rights. This is why a number of Muslim jurists[66] have stated that this verse concerned a very specific case and that consequently it cannot be taken as a source of legislation.

This verse contains another significant example of the Qur'an's progressive approach to the instauration of reforms in favour of the social integration of women. At that time and like a number of other societies around the world, the management of commercial affairs was primarily a man's sphere. Nonetheless, and despite the fact that women were kept away from this domain, the Qur'an advocates their participation and their presence in these sorts of pacts.[67] Via the example of this type of transaction, the Qur'an allowed the Muslim women of the time to make a modest intervention, certainly, but an intervention all the same into the very closed and very masculine world of commercial affairs.

The objective of this verse was, thus, first and foremost to ensure that the female contribution would be effective even if initially it required calling on two women for one man. It is true that some scholars have undertaken a very misogynistic reading and assert that, in this verse, there is tangible evidence of male superiority over women.

But other scholars, such as Ibn Taymiyyah, who understood the objective of the verse, affirm without hesitation that the attestation of a single woman must be accepted if the latter is experienced and familiar with these sorts of transactions. What matters in the Qur'anic vision is, while including women in private economic management, ensuring the protection of people's rights.

This is without doubt what 'Umar ibn al-Khattab had understood in naming, during his caliphate, a woman by the name of Shifa Bint 'Abdallah, as *muhtasib*, which is the current equivalent of the function of a financial controller. In fact, Shifa was charged with controlling financial transactions and ensuring the rectitude

---

66. Among these jurists, there were the older figures, such as Ibn Taymiyya and his disciple Ibn al-Qayyim al-Jawziyya and the contemporaries like Imam Muḥammad 'Abdū and shaykh Muḥammad Shaltūt.

67. Dr Taha Jaber Al-Alwani, *The Testimony of Women in Islamic Law*, www.alhewar.com/TahaTestimony.htm.

of behaviour in commercial centres. This is one example of the application of the Qur'an's directives which the Caliph 'Umar ibn al-Khattab did not hesitate to instate on the ground, shortly after the death of the Prophet.

As for testimony strictly speaking, the Qur'an draws no distinction between that of a woman and that of a man. Shaykh Muḥammad Shaltūt refers to the verse evoking the anathema in the case of adultery and where the testimony of a woman is absolutely equal to that of a man.[68]

As for Ibn al-Qayyim al-Jawziyya, he justifies legal equality in the testimony between a man and a woman by the following verse:

> *And thus have We willed you to be a community of the middle way, so that [with your lives] you might bear witness to the truth before all mankind [...].* (al-Baqarah 2: 43)

The community of which the Qur'an speaks is a community made of men and women and there is no difference between the testimonies of two types of human beings.

Finally, it is important to recall the legal principle in Islam which stipulates that men and women are equal in their transmission of hadith. And, there is no doubt that the transmission of hadith is a form of testimony. If such is the case, how can anyone assert that the testimony of women is accepted as regards the various sayings and actions of the Prophet and rejected when it comes to other people?[69]

Inheritance

The majority of non-Muslims – and many Muslims – have a stereotyped perception of Muslim inheritance law which, in their eyes, can be summed up by one rule: men inherit double that of what women do.

---

68. *Al-Nūr* 24: 6–8.
69. See 'Umarah, op. cit., p. 83.

It is true that there exists a verse in the Qur'an which states:

> CONCERNING *[the inheritance of]* your children, God enjoins *[this]* upon you: The male shall have the equal of two females' share *[...]*. (al-Nisā' 4: 11)

Firstly, it would be interesting to determine the circumstances of the revelation of this verse which, in truth, taken on its own, could seem deeply unfair towards women![1]

The majority of classical commentators state that the verse was revealed when a woman came to find the Prophet to complain that after the death of her husband, her brother had come to take all her and her daughters' possessions. In fact, before the advent of Islam, the Arabs did not recognize any right to inheritance for women or children. They believed that only adult men who took part in wars and the defence of the tribe had a right to inherit. The revelation of this verse – and of all the others concerning inheritance – provoked a profound stir at the heart of the community of the time which could not yet conceive that women, as is the case for children in fact, could benefit from such rights![70]

After the revelation of this verse which, once again, responds to the request of a woman who had come to demand a right – an unthinkable action by the mentality of the time – a widespread social injustice was rectified.

Thus this verse, analysed in the specific context of the time, indicates the extent to which revelation sought to end innumerable arbitrary laws to which the most destitute were subject. What is more, the tremendous confusion which remains around this question of inheritance is that which tends to simplify its application and reduce it to the sole and unique content of this verse. In fact, it is often omitted that this verse only evokes one set of circumstances among many other possibilities in the succession recommended by the Qur'an. The verse in question refers to the specific case of a sister who inherits half of the amount her brother inherits.[J] This is certainly not a general rule, in which case God would have specified

---

70. *Tafsīr* Ibn Kathir.

that in all the cases of inheritance law, man should inherit double the amount women do!

Muslim jurists have in fact asserted that in the Qur'an, inheritance laws depended, among other things, on the closeness of kinship to the deceased person and on the financial responsibility incurred to the inheritor towards other members of his family. This is how there are several possible scenarios regarding inheritance outlined in the Qur'an in which women inherit a greater portion than men (in over ten cases), cases where the woman inherits and the man doesn't, and several cases where the woman inherits the same amount as a man![71]

Inheritance law in Islam is rather complex and cannot be reduced to a single rule. One could take just one example among many other potential possibilities during inheritance to show that the law of dividing up is in a majority of cases blind to gender. Indeed, one could be faced with the case of the death of a man who leaves behind a daughter and both his parents. According to Islamic law, his daughter will receive the greatest share since half the inheritance will be hers, whereas each parent will receive a sixth of the total. The father of the deceased thus receives a smaller portion than that of the daughter and the same amount as his wife.

Outside of the specific verses where it is prescribed to Muslims how to undertake inheritance sharing, there is a verse which promotes a general basic principle concerning laws of inheritance and which states:

> MEN SHALL have a share in what parents and kinsfolk leave behind, and women shall have a share in what parents and kinsfolk leave behind, whether it be little or much - a share ordained [by God]. (al-Nisā' 4: 7)

It is interesting to note how this verse which is supposed to formally

---

71. There are thirty listed cases in which the woman inherits an equal amount or more than the man and only four instances in which she inherits half. See, 'Umarah, op. cit., p. 79. For more details, see the study by Ṣalaḥ ad-Din Sulṭan on women's inheritance in Islam, *Mirath al-Mar'ah wa-Qadiyat al-Musawah*, (Egypt: Dar al-Nahdah, 1999.)

establish the right to inheritance for women in an equal fashion to that for men is often ignored in favour of one which refers to a very specific case.

In the Qur'an, gender is not always taken into account in the case of inheritance except for cases where the financial responsibility is significant, or even entirely incumbent upon the man, as in the example of the verse where the brother inherits twice as much as the sister. In fact, according to Qur'anic principles and with regards to customs of the time, men were required to provide for the needs of their respective families, women, children and elderly included. This logic of additional financial responsibility which is incumbent upon men did not emerge with the advent of Islam, far from it, rather it has always existed across all civilizations. It nonetheless takes, according to the context and the time, different connotations and is interpreted in patriarchal cultures, Mediterranean, Arab and Latin-American, as a type of favouritism afforded to men and which has often translated into veritable patriarchal tyranny.

The Qur'an has indeed insisted on this obligation on men to provide for women's needs – whether they be rich or poor – in several verses and has thus delineated the field of action of this responsibility or *qiwama*, essentially at the heart of the family unit and in a spirit of financial responsibility for the family. This responsibility incumbent upon men should not be understood as a means of subordinating women who would be thus maintained and of seeing in this distinction a discrimination towards women. In fact, could suggest that the Qur'an offers women an additional security in a difficult patriarchal world. To give men a sense of responsibility because women might find themselves unable to manage the economic needs of the family due to pregnancy or other personal reasons, is in fact a favour conceded to women. In the current legal language, the Qur'an displays *positive discrimination* towards women![72]

---

72. 'Azīza al-Hibrī, 'The Rights of Muslim Women in the Global Village: Challenges and Opportunities', p. 113. <http://karamah.org/wp-content/uploads/2011/10/Muslim-Womens-Rights-in-the-Global-Village-Challenges-and-Opportunities.pdf>

Consequently, even when the brother inherits double the amount his sister does, there exists a significant difference between his inheritance and hers. Formulated differently, the amount inherited by the sister is a net sum, in addition to her goods, whereas that inherited by her brother is a gross sum, from which he will have to deduct the expenses of the other people under his responsibility.[73]

Nonetheless, one must concede that the Qur'anic principle of maintenance and financial responsibility, incumbent upon male relatives, are far from being scrupulously respected and sadly remain of the theoretical realm in the day-to-day life of Muslim societies throughout the world. In addition to this, the upheaval experienced at the heart of the great majority of Muslim families, which faced with new socioeconomic realities, are experiencing a real internal imbalance, one can easily imagine the intensity of the damage perpetrated by Qur'anic precepts read through patriarchal lenses!

If the Qur'anic principle itself is immutable since, as we have seen, it advocates first and foremost justice and equality, the economic and social parameters have changed and this requires a re-reading of certain questions arising out of inheritance, in light of the new context in which we find ourselves.

If, in the Qur'an, certain inheritance laws were established with relation to the economic responsibility of men, what are we to make of them today when men are unable to provide alone for the needs of an entire family and where the woman shares the same responsibilities and sometimes even double the load? Women are also maintaining the family when nothing in the texts requires her to do so aside from an increasingly difficult socioeconomic environment and the inability of her husband to decently provide for the needs of an increasingly demanding reality. Should this responsibility for the family, this *qiwama* conditioned in the Qur'an precisely on this responsibility to provide for the needs of the other members of the family, remain an exclusively masculine preserve?

---

73. Ibid., p. 115.

Or should this *qiwamah* be rethought, and in conformity with the spirit of the Qur'anic text, in our wider context, be given a broader and more appropriate significance, namely that of equality?

A *qiwama* of both men and women, both responsible and aware of the importance of responsibilities and obligations which are theirs at the heart of this sensitive and primordial unit which is the family.

It might also be necessary to create new laws which would require men to fulfil their obligations towards women and their families, to think of forms of compensation[74] towards women, abandoned by the entire male hierarchy, husband, brother, uncle. The very same people who are precisely required, according to Islamic principles, to support them psychologically and materially and who generally are only present to impose their alleged masculine superiority and who disappear when it is actually time to assist, to support and provide for the needs of close ones!

Beyond this theoretical reflection on the question of inheritance, necessary but insufficient on its own, urgent measures are needed in order to remain faithful to the principle of justice in the Qur'an and not to perpetrate situations in which the literal application of Qur'anic precepts equates to supporting living conditions replete with injustice and despair. It is necessary to consider means of social compensation for women in order to rebalance the injustices and alleviate the suffering experienced by mothers abandoned to their distress ... Women who find themselves alone, sometimes facing inhuman situations and who, silently, take on the entire responsibility for the family.

The blind application of certain Islamic principles in an unjust and unstructured social context leads to the worst types of discrimination and goes against precisely what the principle is intended to protect!

It should be necessary that the requirement of justice which underpins the laws on inheritance in Islam be manifest in the concrete application on the ground. This is certainly the challenge of the reformist struggle which must, while remaining faithful to

---

74. Suggestion made by Tariq Ramadan.

the spirit of the Qur'an, allow Muslims, men and women, to live their faith and daily life serenely.

Hit them ...?

Is there a passage in the Qur'an which, as is often claimed, justifies the use of violence against women? One can categorically respond no, regardless of the arguments of those who appear convinced by this assumption.

The verse often blamed for 'allowing' husbands to beat their wives – *MEN SHALL take full care of women with the bounties which God has bestowed more abundantly on the former than on the latter, and with what they may spend out of their possessions. And the righteous women are the truly devout ones, who guard the intimacy which God has [ordained to be] guarded. And as for those women whose ill-will you have reason to fear, admonish them [first]; then leave them alone in bed; then beat them [...].* (*al-Nisa'* 4: 34) – begins by outlining men's responsibility, namely the *qiwama* previously evoked, to then refer to a situation of *nushuz*, generally translated as 'insubordination of the wife', and which some scholars have interpreted to mean 'adultery'.[75] Beyond the given explanation by the exegetes concerning the *nushuz*, it is clear that it refers to a situation of major conflict at the heart of the couple.'[76]

The verse continues with directives concerning the manner in which men should behave vis-à-vis this marital problem. In theory, it should unfold in three stages; firstly with an attempt at reconciliation through communication, then the stage of isolation in the marital bed where it is recommended the husband refrain from all physical relations with his spouse as a means of coercion, and finally the stage of *fa-dribuhunna*, literally translated as 'beat her', or 'correct her'.

Before examining the terminology used in this verse, it is worth looking at how and in which context the above

75. Ibn Manzur, *Lisan al-'Arab*.
76. See the detailed study by 'Aziza al-Hibri in, An Islamic Perspective on Domestic Violence *Fordham International Law Journal*, 27/1 (2003): 195–224. (www.karamah.org).

mentioned verse was revealed. The majority of exegetical commentators narrate the stories of women who came to see the Prophet to complain of ill-treatment from their spouses.[77]

Faced with this situation, the Prophet, known for his aversion to all forms of violence against the oppressed and women in particular, reacted sternly by giving the women in question the right to respond according to an eye for an eye or *qiṣāṣ*. The women[78] mistreated by their husbands were permitted by the Prophet of Islam to punish the husband's offence by a treatment of the same order.

A revolutionary response by the standards of the time and which, even today, would be unthinkable! How could one not, based purely on this decision alone, affirm that Islam encouraged equality between men and women within limits inconceivable for a Bedouin, tribal society?!

One can easily imagine the scope of the discontent of the men at the time who were already experiencing a loss of their authority and superiority by accepting to be admonished by their wives in this fashion!

Indeed, the men, deeply scandalized by this solution, came *en mass* to complain to the Prophet, arguing that this would incite all the women to rebel against their husbands.[79]

It was at that moment that the Prophet received the revelation of the verse which appears, therefore, at first glance, to contradict his initial decision! He wanted any mistreatment of women to be formally circumscribed but Divine law apparently had something else in store! This is what the Messenger says when he announces to the others the revelation of the verse in question: '*Muhammad decided one thing and God decided another!*'[80]

In fact, the revelation was merely applying the same, consistent philosophy of gradualism. Taking into account a given primitive

---

77. The most commonly cited version is that of Ḥabibah, wife of Saʿd ibn Rabiʿ who came to complain to the Prophet about the slap she received from her husband, in the *Tafsīr* by Ibn Kathir.
78. *Tafsīr* Ibn Kathir.
79. Ibid.
80. Al-Qurṭbi.

social order, as regards its social vision of women, the Qur'an did not permit the mistreatment of women. Rather, it introduced transitory phases in view of a progressive transformation of people's mind sets. Whereas the Prophet's approach was radical and could have led to reactions of social revolt which would have been difficult to manage within a society in which everything needed to be rebuilt, that of the Creator was certainly different, but seeking to achieve the same objective.

What is more, this verse must be read in light of other verses which refer to marriage and marital relations. The Qur'anic vision of the institution of marriage is a vision based on love, compassion and mutual help. Many verses encourage mutual respect, kindness and tenderness. The Qur'an describes marital relations as a relationship of tranquillity, serenity and affection. A relationship between two people, based on a profoundly intimate connection so beautifully described by the Qur'an which refers to being a 'garment' for one another ... .

> [...] they are as a garment for you, and you are as a garment for them [...]. (al-Baqarah 2: 187)

Each one carrying the skin of the other or dressing oneself with the other like a second skin, each being the alter ego of the other ... .

Or like this other verse which encourages husbands to live with their wives in compassion and kindness or to separate from them with decency.

> [...]either retain them in a fair manner or let them go in a fair manner. [...]. (al-Baqarah 2: 231)

It is interesting to note that this Qur'anic passage which establishes the basis for marital coexistence has been considered by many scholars as being a legal principle in Islamic jurisprudence which stipulates the prohibition of spouses hurting one another: 'la-darar wa-la-dirar'. One finds in the classical books of exegesis that the first Muslims used to insist the formulation of this verse be incorporated into their marriage contract, as a sort of moral protection. This motion can be found in a number of personal statute codes in Muslim countries and a Muslim woman has the right to take legal action against her husband or to divorce him, on the basis of ill treatment.[81]

The Prophet's rejection of all violence against women is recognized by all. Many hadiths denounce the mistreatment of women and condemn acts of violence committed by men. On this topic, the hadiths are too numerous to cite in their entirety but the most well-known are sufficient to perceive the importance which the Prophet attributed to this problem and his intense action to educate Muslims in order that they behave with decency and respect towards their spouses.

'The best among you are those who are best to their wives ... and I am the best among you in this regard.'

This single hadith is sufficient for Muslims who are required to bear in mind the Prophet's lifestyle and to imitate his behaviour and his example.

After gathering a general overview of marital relations according to the Qur'an and the Prophetic tradition, how can one possibly read and interpret the verse *fa-dribuhunna* as 'beat them'?

This question must surely have troubled the majority of scholars, both pre-modern and modern. It is clear to see the extreme precaution, even the difficulty encountered by scholars in their writings, to explain the terminology and in particular, to furnish instructions! Because even though the majority spoke of correcting or striking one's wife, the practical methodology of this correction was reduced to its minimum until ultimately, ending up by symbolising a completely insignificant act.

An example of this is the most common and that most frequently heard interpretation which consists in comparing the action to a touch or a brush with a small, soft stem, like the *miswak*, used as a toothbrush in the Arabic peninsula![82]

---

81. See 'The Rights of Muslim Women in the Global Village' al-Hibrī, p. 127.
82. This interpretation is by Ibn 'Abbās.

Another explanation is offered by the verse which mentions the story of Prophet Job or Ayyub. This Prophet, tested at length, was faced with a real dilemma ... His wife committed an act which had deeply disconcerted him and for which he swore to correct her. Nevertheless, he realized that this act was unworthy of him but, that at the same time, he owed it to himself to respect his oath. A Qur'anic verse offered him the solution to this dilemma:

> *[And finally We told him:] "Now take in thy hand a small bunch of grass, and strike therewith, and thou wilt not break thine oath!* (Ṣād 38: 44)

The objective being to allow Ayyub to respect his oath without all the while wronging his wife.

The symbolic action of the bunch of grass is suggestive of the concept of *non-violence* advocated by the Qur'an. A very suggestive gesture, laden with meaning, which educates Muslims on another way of acting and reacting in the face of the internal impulses of an always latent violent human nature ... .

Faced with all these signs, these preliminary stages, these measures of subtle dissuasion and this Divine pedagogy of non-violence, the scholars ruled in favour of an extreme restriction of this action, to the extent of even abrogating it.

Concerning the term itself of *adribuhunna* 'beat them', the scholars have unanimously concluded a sort of formal consensus advocating the prohibition of all violence against women. They have also, given the Qur'anic ideal of marital relations, concluded that a physically and verbally mistreated woman has the right to request divorce.

Contemporary interpretations also tend to advocate a meaning of *non-violence* as promoted by the Qur'an.

The root *daraba* from which comes *adribuhunna* appears over twenty times in the Qur'an with meanings as different as they are contradictory such as: cover, give, walk, accompany, turn away from, leave, change, take as an example ... One could ask oneself why, concerning this specific verse, the term should take the meaning of 'beat'.[83]

Why should the term not rather mean 'to separate from, physically' and to distance oneself temporarily from one's spouse by living the marital home? In fact, one could assert that the *guiding principle* of the discourse in this verse is more in tune with this meaning since, on closer inspection, the classical interpretation is in fact relatively inconsistent if one follows the reasoning which advocates the three progressive stages, from the easiest to the hardest, in order to resolve a marital conflict. Indeed, after the call to reconcile, the second stage, that of physical isolation from the marital bed, is much more severe than the last which advocates, according to the classical exegeses, a very symbolic punishment ... A wife is far more wounded in her self-esteem by the refusal of her spouse to share her marital bed than by the third stage which actually consists in *brushing* her with a twig!

One might ask if there is not, in fact, a contradiction at the very heart of this widely accepted interpretation? That of leaving the home would be far more logical since it is more serious than physically separating while still sharing the marital bed!

And ultimately we should remain realistic and admit that even if, according to the classical commentary, the act of '*striking*' was symbolic, for those who stop at a literal reading of the texts and who ignore other principles, this is used as a sufficient reason to justify all sorts of mistreatment of their wives!

Is it not legitimate therefore to question the validity of this interpretation, all the more so given that this meaning seems to be in contradiction with the overarching meaning of the Qur'anic message? Compared also with the Prophet's irreproachable behaviour, who was during his lifetime, entirely opposed to all

---

83. The current trend is to interpret the term notably by 'separate from' or 'leave', which corresponds to the attitude of the Prophet who, following a martial dispute, isolated himself for a month from his spouses. See 'Abdel Hamid Ahmad Abu Sulayman, *Darb al-Mar'a Wasila li-Hall al-Khilafat al-Zawjiyyah*, (Cairo: Dar al-Salam, 2002).

forms of restrictions, or physical, or even verbal violence towards women.

This is also another sizeable argument against any religious justification of marital violence. It is intolerable that some Muslims Islamically justify *their right to physically correct their spouse*! The Prophet of Islam never struck nor even lifted a finger against a woman, nor against anyone else for that matter ... Was he not he who was sent to perfect the noble rules of universal morality?!

Can the classical interpretation of 'beat them' thus; retain any of its coherence at the heart of these noble rules of universal morality? Or, would it be wiser to agree, in all humility as the Messenger did in the face of the revelation of this verse, that 'God decided otherwise' by giving this term another significance, a deeper meaning which escapes us and which, perhaps, He alone holds the secret to, but which cannot in any circumstance justify violence, as symbolic as it may be?

CONCLUSION

Islam or the story of an aborted women's revolution
After the advent of Islam, a movement of women's liberation was put in place that shook the social system of the time, which was essentially grounded in a mercilessly patriarchal system.

Encouraged by the Qur'an's directives and the teachings of the Prophet which incited women to *'speak for themselves'*, women entered the social sphere, transgressing tribal laws and seeking to break with humiliating ancestral customs. They entered Islam against the wishes of their family and of the tribal and political power of the time. They contributed in unimaginable ways to the spread of the message, through their sacrifices, their resistance to physical and psychological abuse due to their religious activism. They exiled themselves in the name of their faith ... they allied themselves politically and spiritually with the Messenger ... .

In collaborating side by side with men from the new community, these women spoke up, demanding their rights, participating in all the political action undertaken at the time, they invested themselves materially, physically and morally for the cause of Islam. This is certainly a women's revolution in the heart of the Arabian Desert, where the Qur'anic revelation and the teachings of the Prophet of Islam called on men and women to compete in piety and good deeds. Women, thus, massively took their place at the heart of the mosque with men, in order to educate themselves, to debate and to join in with the decisions being taken by the community. Centuries later, our mosques have become closed spaces, reserved for men whereas women are relegated to cramped spaces, cut off from the rest of the community by walls and opaque curtains. Condemned to exiling themselves this time to the furthest recesses of the centres of learning and power, our Muslim women are resigned, they have accepted submission and worse, have transmitted their renunciation and ignorance to their descendants ... .

A historical survey revealed that at the time of the death of the Prophet there was a scholarly and erudite elite made up of 8,000 people, of which 1,000 were women. The emancipation conveyed by Islam in a quarter of a century meant that one person out of eight of the scholarly elite was a woman. This observation is in itself telling.[1]

How could the earliest Muslim women have acceded to these spaces of freedom, of knowledge and power, fourteen centuries ago in the name of Islam when today they are forbidden access to these same spaces in the name of this same Islam?!

What happened in between that in the name of Islam we allow things which the sacred text and tradition of the Prophet reproved of and sometimes even proscribed?

How can we approve patriarchal customs replacing the sacred text to the point of conveying that the Qur'an itself is a fundamentally patriarchal text! Nothing could be more false than this assertion since, from the beginning of revelation, on the contrary Islam fought against the patriarchal traditions and customs strongly anchored in this region of Arabia.

One can even assert that the Qur'an is an anti-patriarchal text since, in numerous verses, one finds a critique and even a categorical rejection of the main manifestations of patriarchal culture.

Indeed, the Qur'an radically rejects one of the founding elements of patriarchy, namely 'God the male-Father' who perpetuates a real continuity between the Father-God and the male father and the power of which extends to the husband who, through Divine right,

---

1.   Ibn al-Athir and Usd al-Ghāba. See 'Umarah, op. cit.

exercises his power over his wife.[2] This concept of 'God the father' is what is more antithetical to the concept of unicity in Islam.

The Qur'an condemns the sacralisation of Prophets as fathers of their communities and harshly criticizes, in several verses, those who blindly follow the path of their fathers:

> *But when they are told, "Follow what God has bestowed from on high," some answer, "Nay, we shall follow [only] that which we found our forefathers believing in and doing." Why, even if their forefathers did not use their reason at all, and were devoid of all guidance?* (al-Baqarah 2: 170)

The Qur'an has, thus, well and truly denounced this patriarchal power represented by male authority and one cannot accept that in the very name of what Islam denounces, one might endorse discriminatory patriarchal practises.

It is, therefore, astounding to see that the *momentum of liberation* which was started by the last revealed religion was stunted in its path. The discourse on women, as it was formulated by the Qur'an and Sunnah over 1,400 years ago, was resolutely more emancipatory, distinctly different, even at times opposed to that which is put forward today.

Whereas the Qur'an transmitted an egalitarian message with rights and responsibilities, spoke of women in a clear effort to raise them up, responded to their requests, was in conversation with them ... spoke of political participation, of *bay'ah*, of political exile, of social participation, of demanding rights, of freedom of speech ... Today, the bulk of the discourse on women in Islamic rhetoric is focused on abstract and very infantilising moralising concepts.

The woman is a *fitnah*, 'temptation', the woman is '*awrah*' 'illicit' to look at, debates are had on her obligatory return to the home and there is a disproportionate insistence on her dress code and her body.

The majority of the current Islamic discourse on women is

---

2. Asma Barlas, *"Believing Women in Islam": Unreading Patriarchal Interpretations of the Qur'an*, (Austin: University of Texas Press, 2002).

limited to her body; on the most appropriate way to cover, what is permissible or impermissible in terms of clothing, on the prohibition of wearing perfume, of speaking loudly, of laughing! Is this what the message of Islam can be summed up by for women? Where is the liberating spirit of the Qur'an and all the initiatives put forward by the text to initiate a truly autonomous status for women?

It is true that in Islam, as in all monotheistic religions in fact, there is an ethic of behaviour and fundamental values of *decency* as regards the body, to be followed and respected. But, too often we forget that the rules of physical decency pertain to men just as much as they do to women. And, one cannot reduce the core of the spiritual message to a dress code, like the recurring question of the veil, and to perpetual discourses on the dangers of female temptation and on themes overly focused on women's bodies. The veil has become a priority, even the *absolute priority* for all self-respecting Muslim women, and some Muslim women, in donning the veil, reduce the core of their demands to this action which, due to its constant repetition, loses credibility and becomes an empty slogan, derisory in the face of weightier demands. Beyond the Qur'anic prescription of the veil (the Qur'an speaks of *khimar*) which can neither be imposed nor forbidden since in both cases this would reflect a totalitarian logic, it is up to women and women alone to choose whether to wear it or not, and not to anyone else! This veil, alleged symbol of female oppression for some, has become through the media frenzy and a consistent ideological construction, the veritable symbol of a foil which generates in the West, just as in Muslim lands, deeply passionate responses!

Finally, it is the same type of discourse which we find here on either side. On one hand, the one who wishes to *free* women from this Islam which oppresses them – which covers them a little too much – and which remains obsessed, in another way, by women's bodies which it wishes in this case to *un-cover*. On the other hand, there are those who focus the core of the spiritual message around women's bodies which require being *over-covered* because the female body represents in itself the *visibility* of Islam, as an identity which requires preserving and the veil sums up in itself the entire moral of Islam ... .

In both cases, and with few differences between them, we are facing a sexist ideology which ignores women's intelligence, which overlooks her human dignity and her personal capacity to make her own choices in the name of her convictions.

The spirit of this process of *liberation* undertaken by the revelation has, thus, been subverted and the impulse experienced by this question of the Muslim woman has been gradually eroded in favour of a jurisdiction which has persisted in closing all openings, as much within the Qur'anic orientations as in the Prophetic tradition.

The philosophy of *gradualism* advocated by the Qur'an which, among others, sought a progressive liberation and emancipation of women, has been ignored, which has favoured the regression of women's status.

Women's revolution was, therefore, rapidly aborted and discriminatory patriarchal customs swiftly gained the upper hand, directing the religious discourse towards a restriction of acquired freedoms, in the name of a religious morality emptied of its quintessence.

The decadence of the Muslim world was accompanied inevitably by an even more pronounced decadence of women's status due to two great tragedies.

First, that of the multiple conflicts inherent to autocratic power and then to the persistence of slavery. Whereas the Qur'an outlines several times the dispositions for the gradual abolition of slavery in declaring all acts of liberation as rewardable, Muslims have for centuries allowed this practise to persist, which as it concerns women, contributed to the institutionalising their confinement in harems.

And for centuries, whereas the door to *ijtihād* was closed – an indispensable tool for the evolution of Islamic thought – the door to legal speculation was opened, as in the case of *sadd adh-dharā'i'*, an actual legal provision which has largely contributed to institutionalising the official culture of women's subordination. Conceived as a veritable *preventative code*, in other words, *a code of fear*, its content has been, at least as concerns women's status, extremely repressive, even as it is clear that certain scholars have elaborated this type of *code* in an effort to preserve their respective societies from any potential moral depravity. Nonetheless, the result has undeniably been overreach and very constraining laws concerning the Islamic gains in areas of law and freedoms for women. This is how we experience many laws forbidding some of the most elementary rights in Islam in the name of *sadd adh-dharā'i'*. Such as the right to education and to knowledge which were denied to women for a long time in the name of protecting social mores and moral rules! Yet when we deny women the right to knowledge, we are denying them the right to justice and in both cases we find ourselves in flagrant contradiction with the basic principles of Islam.

Developing these sorts of legal rulings which advocate all manner of prohibitions[3] in order to protect again the unavoidable risks of a depravation of mores, is proof that our thinking is fatally *besieged*! In addition to being the easy way out, it is an approach which testifies to the intellectual abdication of our Islamic system of thought, incapable of confronting the real problems of our society. It is not a question of *prohibiting* out of anticipation but rather of *educating* in order to awaken the search for meaning and conscience, which alone can protect us against immorality and all sorts of debauchery. It is a question of developing a true ethic of the management of freedoms through an appropriate spiritual education which takes into account the subtle realities of each context.

Those among the scholars who used this preventative concept of *sadd adh-dharā'i'* rigorously were surely trying, in good faith, to mould the Islamic community, in order to reach an assumed *idealized Islamic state*. But, this is of the order of a utopia because even during the Prophet's lifetime there was no ideal Islamic community!

---

3. See the list of prohibitions made law in the name of this principle in Abu Shuqqah, *Taḥrir al-Mar'a fī 'Ahd ar-Risala*, 4th edition, (Cairo: Dar al-Qalam, 1995).

This is, what is more, an impossibility on the scale of human reality. God wanted human diversity to be a basic principle in this life and even a true test. He wanted human society to be one in which good exists alongside bad, where good confronts evil, where good works against the bad or the less good ... .

Our life on earth is not that of angels who are perfect beings, living in a perfect world. Our life is that of all human experiences... made up of constraints and successes, failures and torments, tragedies and joys, happiness and sadness, to test our endurance, our resistance, our faith and our submission. How can we deal with this reality with static and frozen doctrines, a thousand miles from our daily concerns?

How do we confront the complexity of our social realities when we remain prisoners of laws which, in addition to having been devised in radically different contexts, are at times in total contradiction with the driving principles of the Qur'anic message?

How do we revive this spirit of liberation advocated by the Islam of revelation but stifled in the confines of an Islamic history which remains in a horrifying silence?

How do we revive this impulse in the heart of Muslims, especially in the heart of Muslim women, who as women, are the first to be affected by this denial of justice?

How can we convince those who seem to resist this entire movement of reformism through fear of losing themselves?

How can we explain to them that, in fact, we cannot remain faithful to Islam without renewal, without a critical conscience, without deep reflection and constructive debate?

The objective of this book is not to claim to have answered all of these questions. The idea is to participate in a limited way in this debate of ideals concerning Islamic renewal.

To suggest a re-reading of the sources and of its interpretations from a feminine perspective is not the only solution to the problems experienced by women in Islamic societies.

But, is it not said that speaking up is already a way of taking action? That is what I have sought to do in this book... in all humility.

God is my witness ...

GLOSSARY OF TERMS

Abyssinia – The ancient name for modern Ethiopia.

Ahad hadith – An isolated Hadith with a single *isnad* (transmission chain).

Ahl al-hadith – Lit., 'People of Hadith', Muslim sect who place emphasis on hadith literature.

Al-hanif – 'Primordial monotheist', a title given to Prophet Abraham.

Al-kayd – 'The deception' or, 'the act of trickery'.

Aya(h) – Lit., 'a sign', but understood as a verse from the Qur'an.

Bayt at-taa – The residence of obedience.

Fiqh – Islamic jurisprudential laws.

Furussiya – Excellent equestrian skills or, horsemanship.

Hadith – (pl., Ahadith), Narration of the Prophet Muhammad.

Hijra(h) – The Prophet's migration, from Makkah to Madinah.

Ijtihād – An exerted struggle, to come to an Islamic jurisprudential ruling.

Ishārāt – Textual implication.

Jibril – The Archangel Gabriel.

Kaba (Kaabah) – Lit., 'cube', the square edifice at the centre of the sanctified mosque in Makkah.

Khalifah – Lit., 'representative' or, 'vicegerent', but understood as the leader of the Muslim community (Caliph).

Ma'rūf – Well-known or, generally accepted knowledge.

Madyan – Lit., 'square', but understood to be the centre of a city or town.

Safa and *Marwa* – The two small hillocks situated beside the Kaabah.

Mubahalah – Permitted action, without sin or reward.

Mubayiʿat/bayʿah – Something given under oath/oath of allegiance.

Muhajirat – (sing., *Muhajarah*) Females who migrated to Madinah with the Prophet.

Muharraran – Freed from the slavery of this world.

Nafs – 'The lower self' or, 'reproachable self'.

Niyya(h) – Intention.

Nushūz – Insubordination or, disobedience of a wife.

Pact of al-Hudaybiyya(h) – A place south of Makkah where the first Muslim converts of Madinah pledged their allegiance to Islam.

Qiṣāṣ – Retaliation.

Qiwama – Gaurdianship.

Qur'an – Lit., 'The Recitation', the divine message given to Prophet Muhammad.

Quraysh – The leading tribe of Makkah during Muhammad's era.

Rizq – Sustenance.

Sadd ad-dharāʾiʿ – A legal preventative code to block undesired consequences.

Shahādah – Martyrdom or, witnessing one's faith.

Surah – Chapter of the Qur'an.

Ṭāʿa – Obedience.

Tafsīr – (pl., *Tafasir*) Exegesis/exegeses of the Qur'an.

Taklīf – Obligation.

Taradi – Common agreement.

Tashawur – The Act of consultation.

Tashrif – To be honoured or, respected.

Tawḥīd – The unicity of God/oness.

The Battle of Uhud – A small mountain outside Madinah, the scene of a very important battle during Muhammad's Prophetic mission.

ʿUlema – (sing., *ʿAlim*) Lit., 'Those with knowledge', but understood as Islamic religious scholars.

Zamzam – Spring water situated inside the centre of the sanctified mosque in Makkah.

Zawj – Marital spouse.

PUBLISHERS END NOTES

Lamrabet's sweeping judgements regarding "traditionalist" understanding of Islam, by which she seems to be referring to the scholastic tradition of the past fourteen hundred years, are unfortunately not always substantiated in her work. Rather they are left as broad claims. This does not do a great deal to make her case compelling. In attempting to remedy this somewhat, we have included some endnotes. In some instances, we have not been able to substantiate a claim she has made, or have ourselves found it wanting. In such cases, we note such a concern in the endnote.

A. Perhaps an example that would support her claim, if to a degree, would be that of discouraging and at times prohibiting women from praying in the mosque in the mainstream Hanafi school. This is justified on the basis of the Prophetic tradition informing us that women's prayer is better at home, but the mainstream Hanafi position subsequently evolved and remained for centuries one of more or less forbidding women from attending prayer in the mosque. For a detailed discussion and powerful critique of the restrictive position, see Mohammad Akram Nadwi, *Lawfulness of Women's Prayer in the Mosque*, (Interface Publications, 2015).

B. Such a position is actually adopted by the Syrian hadith master, Shu'ayb al-Arna'ut (b. 1928). Although this is undoubtedly a minority position within the scholarly tradition, al-Arna'ut argues that the authentic hadiths collection doesn't state that Eve was created from Adam's rib. Rather, he professes that the authentic traditions state that a woman is *like* a rib. He contends that commentators drew on the Biblical stories to develop the notion that Eve was created from Adam. The soul (*nafs*) that this and other verses talk about should be understood as neither male or female. See his full comments in al-Nawawi, *Riyad al-Salihin*, ed. Shu'ayb al-Arna'ut, 3rd ed., (Beirut: Mu'assasah al-Risalah, 2001), p. 119, n. 2. As for

'Abduh's interpretation of the verse, for which Lamrabet does not provide a reference, in which the *nafs* is viewed as female. This does not appear to have any other support in the tradition; and as presented by Lamrabet, seems linguistically implausible.

C. According to Ibn Kathir's *Tafsir*, the *mubahalah* incident, alluded to in the Qur'an (Al-'Imran 3: 61), does not in fact call for *all* the members of the community to join, as Lamrabet suggests. Rather it is specifically directed to the Prophet and some close family members. The narratives reported by Ibn Kathir further specify the family members as the Prophet's daughter Fatimah, his cousin and son-in-law 'Ali, and their two sons, Hasan and Husayn. For further details, see Ibn Kathir, *Tafsir al-Qur'an al-'Azim*, ed. Sami b. Muhammad Salamah, (Riyadh: Dar Taybah, 1997), vol. 2, pp. 49-55.

D. The narrations reported in Ibn Kathir's *Tafsir* do not seem to suggest that they are in any way incomplete, hence it seems unwarranted to expect that there were any other people present aside from the four close family members mentioned in the previous footnote.

E. The superiority of men over women was indeed simply assumed to be the case for much of human history in most civilizations. Islamic civilization in general also held this to be the case until very recent times. However in Islamic tradition women have never been regarded as inferior creatures.

This is represented in Ibn Kathir's *Tafsir* which is viewed as an authoritative classical reference work in the genre. Ibn Kathir states in his commentary on the verse of *qiwamah* (al-Nisa 4: 34):

> God says, "Men are caretakers (*qawwamun*) of women." [This] means: man is a caretaker (*qayyim*) of a woman. He is her leader (*ra'is*), her superior (*kabir*), the one in authority over her (*al-hakim 'alay-ha*), and the one who disciplines her when she becomes crooked. [God continues,] "due to what We have preferred some of them over others with." [This is because] men are superior to (*afdal min*) women, and men are better than (*khayr min*) women. For this reason Prophethood is the prerogative of men, and similarly supreme rulership, as the Prophet, peace and blessings be upon him, said "a people who render their affairs [of governance] to a woman cannot prosper." Narrated by Bukhari [...]. The same is the case of the post of a judge. [God continues,] "and due to what they spend of their wealth on them." That is, in terms of dowers, expenditures, and responsibilities that God has placed upon [men] with respect to [women] in His Book and the Sunnah of His Prophet, peace and blessings be upon him. For man is superior to (*afdal min*) woman in and of himself, and he has a rank above her, and he provides for her. Therefore it is appropriate for him to be her caretaker. As God, Most High, says, "men have a degree over [women]." (al-Baqarah 2: 228)

This undoubtedly sounds patriarchal in the extreme to many modern Muslims, but to describe it as an "erroneous" understanding, as Lamrabet does, is anachronistic. This was the prevailing understanding of such verses for much of Islamic history, and new understandings can displace past understandings, but do not necessarily render past ones "erroneous." Of course, translating it as such today is controversial, and for many Muslims, rightly so. Sadly, the English translation widely available for the *Tafsir* deliberately elides or tones down the forthrightness of Ibn Kathir's patriarchal outlook—an outlook that would have been shared by most of his medieval peers. In doing so, the English speaking reader is presented with a bowdlerized version of what Ibn Kathir actually states in his *tafsir*.

F. No source is provided for this claim. It does not seem to have a scholarly basis, but may rather be based on her personal experiences. Hence, it is probably not possible to find a written source.

G. Lamrabet's stance on polygamy is probably one that would find support among many modern Muslims, but only appears to have emerged in modern times. Pre-modern Muslims do not seem to have questioned the right of a Muslim man to marry up to four wives concurrently. It appears apologetic arguments justifying polygamy on the grounds that there was a relative surplus of women due to wars did not emerge until the modern period. The most that can be said about the pre-modern tradition is that some scholars, such as those of the Hanbali school of law, consider taking more than one wife to be legally disliked (*makruh*). This, they argue, is due to the inevitability of a polygamous husband's not being able to realize equal fairness with respect to all his wives, as noted by Lamrabet's Qur'anic citations (al-Nisa 4: 29). See, for example, 'Ala al-Din al-Mardawi, *al-Insaf fi Ma'rifat al-Rajih min al-Khilaf*, eds. al-Hulw and al-Turki, (Cairo: Hajar, 1993), vol. 20, p. 25-27. To suggest that polygamy should be treated like slavery and abolished, however, is a step no pre-modern Muslims ever suggested. The vast majority of modern Muslims do not consider a complete rejection of polygamy acceptable, since it is permitted in the Qur'an, was practised by the Prophet, the four Rightly Guided Caliphs, and large numbers of the pious predecessors. In a sense, however, these are the culture wars that modern Muslims wage in the shadow of Western modernity. Lamrabet draws a parallel here with Tariq Ramadan's controversial call for a moratorium on the corporal punishments prescribed in the Qur'an. Being grounded in the Qur'an, however, calls to bring such practices to an end seem extremely difficult for modern Muslims to scripturally justify. The institution of polygamy is neither *fard* nor *wajib* (compulsory) that every Muslim should aspire for and practise. This is a permission with strict conditions and could be undertaken, if required, by mutual consent.

H. In making her argument about female testimony, Lamrabet draws on the prolific and respected Egyptian scholar, Muhammad 'Umarah (sometimes vocalized 'Imarah) 'Umarah in turn is drawing on a well-known discussion of Ibn al-Qayyim and his teacher Ibn Taymiyyah. The fuller scholarly discussion may be found in Arabic in 'Umarah's work cited by Lamrabet in this section. There is also the article of Mohammad Fadel, "Two Women, One Man: Knowledge, Power, and Gender in Medieval Islamic Legal Thought," *International Journal of Middle East Studies*, Vol. 29, No. 2 (May, 1997), pp. 185-204. Ibn al-Qayyim and Ibn Taymiyyah's views that consider the probative value of female testimony are not, however, widely shared in other schools of thought. The critique of these other schools on this issue should take place on substantive grounds, not on the basis of casting aspersions against those schools with which one disagrees by calling their interpretations "extremely reductive" and "totally erroneous."

I. It is highly inappropriate for any Muslim to suggest, even slightly, that there may be unfairness associated with God's revelation. Hence, characterizing verses on inheritance as seeming to be "deeply unfair towards women" is extremely problematic to say the least. Muslim scholars have historically shown the utmost respect to the scriptural sources themselves, even if the same scholars' interpretations of these scriptures have often allowed them to depart from the apparent meaning of these scriptures.

J. The author's discomfort appears to be based on a misunderstanding of the verses in question. There are two instances in which the Qur'an states that "the male shall have the equal of two females' share", namely al-Nisa 4: 11 and 4: 176. Both are explicitly speaking about the relative shares of sibling offspring, as is made clear by the immediate antecedent clauses in the two verses. Such relative share portioning does not apply to the case of, for example, a mother, or a wife, vis-a-vis her siblings, as Lamrabet seems to understand.

BIBLIOGRAPHY

Qur'an and Commentaries

Ibn Kathīr, *Tafsīr*.

Fakhr ar-Rāzī, *Tafsīr al-kabīr, mafātīḥ al-ghayb*.

Al Qurṭubī, *Al-Jami' li-aḥkām al-qur'ān*.

Ibn 'Abbās, *Tafsir Ibn 'Abbās*, Dar al-kitāb al-'ilmiya, éditions 2000, Beyrouth.

Az-Zamakhsharī, *Al-Kashaf*.

Sayyid Quṭb, *Fī-ẓilāl al-Qur'ān*.

Ibn Kathīr, *Tafsīr*, Dar Al-Kutub al-'ilmiyya, Liban, 2007.

Al-Qushayri, *Tafsīr*.

Sahl at-Tustari, *Tafsīr al-Qur'an al-'azim* (dans l'étude de Pierre Lory).

Rashīd Ridā, *Tafsīr al-Manar*.

Al-Baydāwī, *Tafsīr*.

Le Noble Coran, nouvelle traduction française du sens de ses versets, par Muḥammad Chiadmi, éditions Tawhid, 2004.

Arabic sources

Muḥammad Rashīd Ridā, *Tafsīr al-Manâr*, Dar al-kitâb al-'ilmiyya, Liban, 1999, en arabe.

Riffat Hassan, *L'égalité entre hommes et femmes*, Université de Louisville, Kentucky, www.études-musulmanes. com.

Rachid al-Ghannouchi, *Al mar'a bayna al-Qur'ān wa wāqi' al-muslimīn*, Maghreb center for Researchs and translations, 2000, Londres.

Asmā Ahmed Zyada, 2001, *Dawr al-mar'a as-siyāsī fi 'ahd an-nabi wa al-khulafā' ar-rashidīn*. Éditions Dar as-salam, 2001, en arabe. Étude faite à l'université du Caire pour l'obtention du doctorat en sciences islamiques.

Al-Haytami, *Majma'a azawa'id wa manba' al-fawā'id*.

Tabarī, *Tārīkh al-umam wal mulūk*, Dar Sader, Beyrouth, 2003.

Abū Shuqqa, Voir *Taḥrir al-mar'a fi 'asr ar-risāla*, édition Dar al-Qalam, Koweit, 4e édition, 1995.

Al-Qushayrī, *Lata'if al-ishārāt*, Dar Al-kutub al-'ilmiyya, Beyrouth 2001.

Amina Ameziane el Hassani, *Umm Salama Umm al-mu'minīn*, éditions du ministère des habous et affaires religieuses, Maroc.

INDEX